JOHN O'SHEA

"He has not consciously sought the calm, restrained and beautifully composed in nature. One feels the creative force at work in all he did. The results are almost overpowering at times, but invariably awaken a positive reaction in the observer."

A review of the John O'Shea Memorial Exhibition, Carmel, *Monterey Peninsula Herald*, probably October 1, 1956.

John O'Shea, 1876–1956: The Artist's Life As I Know It

With a complete catalogue of the artist's known works

by
Walter A. Nelson-Rees

Dust jacket illustrations:
 front: POINT LOBOS TREES, detail of plate 134.
 back: BANANA FOLIAGE, *ca.* 1928, plate 95.

Frontispiece. NOTLEY'S LANDING, *ca.* 1931, cat. no. 76. See page 75.

Copyright © 1985 by WIM
6000 Contra Costa Road
Oakland, California 94618
Telephone: (415) 547-0193

All Rights Reserved

No part of this publication may be reproduced, stored in a retrieval system, or transmitted in any form by any means, electronic, mechanical, photocopying, or otherwise, without the prior written permission from the copyright owner, except by a reviewer who wishes to quote brief passages in connection with a review written for inclusion in a magazine, newspaper, or broadcast.

Library of Congress Number: 85:50075

Designed by Gordon Chun
Printed in Japan through Toppan Printing Co. (America) Inc., San Francisco
Typography by Terry Robinson & Company

Photography by Walter A. Nelson-Rees, except where acknowledged otherwise.

ISBN 0-938842-05-6

Contents

9   FOREWORD by Joseph Armstrong Baird, Jr.

13   JOHN O'SHEA, 1876-1956:
THE ARTIST'S LIFE AS I KNOW IT

141   EPILOGUE

144   POSTSCRIPT

146   NOTES

154   BIBLIOGRAPHY

CATALOGUE OF WORKS BY JOHN O'SHEA
156   I. Known Works
166   II. Unlocated Works

171   MEMBERSHIP AND INSTITUTIONAL COLLECTIONS

172   CHRONOLOGY OF JOHN O'SHEA'S LIFE

174   CERTIFICATE OF AUTHENTICITY AND
ESTATE STAMPS

176   AFTERWORD AND ACKNOWLEDGMENTS

"... I spoke of his brilliant directness of handling, the charm of his color and the luminous freshness of his tone quality—also of how happy were his suggestions of the elusive subtleties of atmosphere."

Beatric de Lack Krombach, *Graphic*, February 13, 1915.

1. EUCALYPTUS TREES IN STORM (REVELRY, *ca.* 1915), Coll. Mrs. Warren M. Hussey, cat. no. 41. Photograph courtesy Robert Godfrey, American Visuals, Inc., Terre Haute, Indiana.

*To Molly Jeppson
whose memory of "Uncle John"
started the project, and
Jim Coran whose work
and unselfish devotion
saw it through, and to
Jane Newhall whose support
made it possible*

8

2

"If O'Shea goes on a color spree, it is no more to be condemned than if Ritschel goes on a dramatic spree with his pounding seas of Titanic proportions, or Hansen builds up one of his overwhelming sea scenes."

Francis L. Lloyd, *Carmel Pine Cone*, August 26, 1938.

2. COLORFUL HIGHLANDS, cat. no. 26.

174

". . . he showed a room full of magnificently reckless paintings affirming the savage beauty of desert mountains . . ."

Arthur Millier, *The Argus*, March 1928.

173. CALIFORNIA HILLS, cat no. 16.

174. SHADOWS, cat. no. 101.

175. Edward Hopper, CAPE ANN GRANITE, 1928, oil on canvas, 29″ × 40¼″. Photograph courtesy Sotheby's, New York.

175

POSTSCRIPT

An extraordinary story was recently told us. It may have been known to John O'Shea; if not, it is likely he would have enjoyed it anyway. Molly and John never had children. However, it is said that a year before she married Walter Shaughnessy in 1906, Molly had a "miscarriage," or more accurately, a baby-out-of-wedlock fathered by Shaughnessy. As an infant, the baby girl was given to and cared for by Molly's sister, Emma, Mrs. Benjamin Pine, John O'Shea's future sister-in-law. The girl, raised as Mary Frances Pine, is today Mrs. Warren M. Hussey of Terre Haute, Indiana, and her daughter, Molly, Mrs. Richard M. Jeppson of Carmel and Palm Desert, California, thus appears to be John O'Shea's step-granddaughter (as well as his great niece)!

During the years since O'Shea's death, it was first Emma Pine and then Molly Jeppson who guarded and later had professionally stored the paintings which remained in the artist's last home in Carmel Woods. It is from the latter that WIM Fine Arts, Oakland, California, purchased the bulk of the estate in 1983.

"Whether you like it or not, O'Shea's deep indigo mood in 'The Cove' with its gloomy treatment of that sparkling, happy China Cove at Point Lobos, strikes a rich note . . ."

Francis L. Lloyd, *Carmel Pine Cone*, August 26, 1938.

176. BLUE COVE, DARK CLIFFS, cat. no. 134.

177. SHORELINE AND COAST HILLS THROUGH ROCKS, cat. no. 207.

DOWN THE COAST, detail of plate 26. Photographer unknown.

344. For a brief discussion of this organization see Donald Whitton and Robert Johnson, *Percy Gray*, p. 81.

345. Joseph A. Baird, Jr., "Introduction," in E to E, p. 7.

346. Letter from John O'Shea to Emma Pine, December 20, 1943.

347. SFC, *This Week*, March (?), 1942, p. 12.

348. CPC, February 17, 1928, p. 14; October 29, 1937.

349. Letter from Richard Criley to author dated August 27, 1984.

350. Letter from Ella Young to Emma Pine dated January 6, 1944.

351. MPH, November 1, 1946. See also ns. 7 and 113.

352. Telephone conversation with Jeramyn Davern, Grand Central Galleries, New York City, February 1, 1985.

353. One letter each from Shelley M. Bennett, dated March 28, 1984, and Thomas V. Lange, May 7, 1984, indicate that this work by John O'Shea is not in the collection of the Huntington Library.

354. Patricia Cunningham, "Discriminating Art Lovers Will Derive Much Pleasure from O'Shea Black and White Show at Gallery." No date, no source, but surely June 1945. See n. 291.

355. MPH, November 2, 1953, p. A 2.

356. MPH, November 1, 1946; October 31, 1947; October 29, 1948; October 31, 1949; October 31, 1950.

357. CPC, June 1, 1922.

358. A catalogue is preserved in the Archives of California Art, The Oakland Museum.

359. The lithograph and letter are preserved with the O'Shea scrapbook.

360. The person making this and several other pertinent comments about John O'Shea knew him well, but wished to remain anonymous (July 8, 1984).

361. An undated postcard, probably at Christmas 1954 or 1955.

362. Personal communication from Kent Seavey, Pacific Grove, Calif., October 1984.

363. MPH, November 5, 1951, p. 14.

364. *Robert Henri, Painter*, p. 65.

365. Ibid., pp. 65, 73.

366. Letter from Ella Young to Shawn, dated May 13, 1945.

367. Edith DeShazo, *Everett Shinn*, p. 185.

368. MPH, March 8, 1955.

369. CPC, October 20, 1928.

370. Personal communication from Rose Ulman, November 1984, and listing in Helen Spangenberg, *Yesterday's Artists on the Monterey Peninsula*, p. 49.

371. This painstaking work is being done by Anthony R. White, Hillsborough, Calif.

372. Certificate of Death, State File number 36180, from County Recorder of Monterey County, copy dated February 22, 1984.

373. MPH, April 30, 1956; May 3, 1956; *Terre Haute Star*, May 4 and 5, 1956; CPC, May 3, 1956.

374. Letter from Mrs. Devine, "Your only sister Alice" to "Dear Brother John" (John J. O'Shea), dated August 29, 1940; letter from "Your loving nephew John J. Devine" to "Dear Uncle John" (John J. O'Shea), dated August 15, (no year), most likely 1956; letter from "Your Loving Nephew John J. Devine" to "Dear Mrs. Payne [sic]," dated January 16, 1957. The contents of these three letters indicate that John O'Shea himself had written very infrequently, if at all, to either his sister Alice or her son John J. Devine in the period preceding 1940 ("wrote to you twice but got no answer") and before he died in April 1956 ("I have written many a time and has [sic] failed to receive an answer").

375. Letter from Richard Lofton to Emma Pine dated November 2, 1956.

376. See *The Preston Morton Collection of American Art*, p. 228, where Brian O'Doherty, "Portrait: Edward Hopper," *Art in America* 52 (December 1964): 69 is cited for this quotation.

377. John Canady, "Stranger in a Strange Land," *Focus*, p. 33.

378. *Robert Henri, Painter*, p. 87.

379. The identity of the sitter, of whom O'Shea painted three large pictures, remains unknown. Three persons have come to mind. Abdul Baha, the leader of Bahaism, who visited the United States in 1912 and of whom Molly Shaughnessy (O'Shea) was sent a photograph from Acco (present-day Ákko, Israel), in 1921, shows considerable resemblance. George William Russell (Æ), who visited the O'Sheas in 1930, is another possibility; a stronger likeness is that of Irish orator John O'Leary, as indicated recently by Ethna Waldron (April 12, 1985).

BIBLIOGRAPHY

Albronda, Mildred. "Granville Redmond: California Landscape Painter." *Art and Antiques* 5 (November–December 1982): 46–53.

Art Exhibition by California Artists, exhibition catalogue. San Francisco: Golden Gate International Exposition, California Building, 1939.

Art Exhibition by California Artists, exhibition catalogue. San Francisco: Golden Gate International Exposition, California Building, 1940. (Illustrations of Works of Committee and Jury Members.)

Artists of the Monterey Peninsula, 1875–1925, exhibition catalogue. Monterey, Calif.: Monterey Peninsula Museum of Art, 1981.

Baird, Joseph A., Jr., ed. *From Exposition to Exposition: Progressive and Conservative Northern California Painting, 1915–1939*, exhibition catalogue. Sacramento, Calif.: Crocker Art Museum, 1981.

Bostick, Daisy F., and Castelhun, Dorothea. *Carmel at Work and Play*. Monterey, Calif.: Angel Press, 1977 (a reprint, copyright Lacy Williams Faia, of 1925 publication).

Bridgwater, William, and Sherwood, Elizabeth J., eds. *The Columbia Encyclopedia*. New York: Columbia University Press, 1950.

Brown, Milton, W. *American Painting from the Armory Show to the Depression*. Princeton, New Jersey: Princeton University Press, 1955.

Burnside, Wesley M. *Maynard Dixon, Artist of the West*. Provo, Utah: Brigham Young University Press, 1974.

Canaday, John. "The Lonely Vision of Edward Hopper, Stranger in a Strange Land." *Focus* 28 (December 1981): 12, 31 (reprinted from *Smithsonian*.)

Crocker Art Museum Handbook of Paintings. Sacramento, Calif.: Crocker Art Museum, 1979.

Dawdy, Doris O. *Artists of the American West*. Chicago: The Swallow Press, Inc., 1974.

Del Monte Revisited, exhibition catalogue. Carmel, Calif.: Carmel Museum of Art, 1969.

De Shazo, Edith. *Everett Shinn, 1876–1953, A Figure in His Time*. New York: Clarkson N. Potter, Inc., 1974.

Exhibition of Paintings by John O'Shea, exhibition catalogue. New York: The Kingore Galleries, 1921.

Exhibition of Paintings by John O'Shea, Subjects of Mexico, exhibition catalogue. Monterey, Calif.: Del Monte Art Gallery, 1936.

Exhibition of Paintings in Water Color by John O'Shea, Subjects of California and Mexico, exhibition catalogue. Monterey, Calif.: Del Monte Art Gallery, 1940.

Fielding, Mantle. *Dictionary of American Painters, Sculptors and Engravers*. Enlarged edition. Genevieve C. Doran, ed. Green Farms, Conn.: Modern Books and Crafts, Inc., 1974.

Gerdts, William H. *American Impressionism*. New York: Abbeville Press, 1984.

Hart, James D. *A Companion to California*. New York: Oxford University Press, 1978.

Hensel, Margaret. "Martin Flavin." *Game and Gossip* 5 (May 2, 1952): 2, 33.

Homer, William Innes. *Robert Henri and His Circle*. Ithaca, N.Y.: Cornell University Press, 1969.

Korb, Edward L. *A Biographical Index to California and Western Artists*. Lawndale, Calif.: Old Master Gallery Press, 1983.

Luhan, Mabel Dodge. *Taos and Its Artists*. New York: Duel, Sloan and Pierce, 1979.

Maurice Prendergast, Art of Impulse and Color, exhibition catalogue. College Park, Maryland: University of Maryland, 1976.

"May Loan Exhibition, John O'Shea." *News Flashes* 3 (May 1937): 1 (a pamphlet from the William Rockhill Nelson Gallery of Art, Atkins Museum of Fine Arts, Kansas City, Missouri).

Mead, Katherine H., ed. *The Preston Morton Collection of American Art*. Santa Barbara, Calif.: Santa Barbara Museum of Art, 1981.

Mc Grath, Virginia. "Burton Shepard Boundey." *Game and Gossip* 5 (May 2, 1952): 5, 35.

———. "John O'Shea." *Game and Gossip* 5 (May 2, 1952): 15, 37.

Monterey: The Artist's View, 1925–1945, exhibition catalogue. Monterey, Calif.: Monterey Peninsula Museum of Art, 1982.

Morris Graves: Vision of the Inner Eye, exhibition catalogue. Washington, D.C.: George Brazilier, Inc., New York, in association with The Phillips Collection, Washington, D.C., 1983.

Moure, Nancy D. W. *Dictionary of Art and Artists in Southern California Before 1930*. Los Angeles: privately printed, 1975. (Revised edition, 1984, carries J. O'Shea's death date.)

———. *Painting and Sculpture in Los Angeles, 1900–1945*, exhibition catalogue. Los Angeles: Los Angeles County Museum of Art, 1980.

Munich and American Realism in the 19th Century, exhibition catalogue. Sacramento, Calif.: E. B. Crocker Art Gallery, 1978.

Nelson, Mary C. *The Legendary Artists of Taos*. New York: Watson-Guptill Publications, 1980.

Newhall, Nancy, ed. *The Daybooks of Edward Weston, Volume II. California*. New York: Aperture, n.d.

O'Brien, Frederick J. *White Shadows in the South Seas*. New York: The Century Company, 1920.

Official Art Exhibition, California Pacific International Exposition, exhibition catalogue. San Diego, Calif.: The Palace of Fine Arts, 1935.

Orr-Cahall, Christina, ed. *The Art of California, Selected Works from the Collection of The Oakland Museum*. Oakland, Calif.: The Oakland Museum Art Department, 1984.

Paul Dougherty, A Retrospective Exhibition, exhibition catalogue. Portland, Oregon: Portland Museum of Art, 1978.

Paintings by John O'Shea, exhibition catalogue. San Francisco: The Helgesen Gallery, 1919.

Foreword

John O'Shea represents a special breed of artist—one who appears almost fully developed in his technical powers in a particular place at a particular time. In a real sense, he is the quintessential embodiment of a California artistic phenomenon—the Carmel area artist of the period between World War I and World War II. After a short period of training in the eastern United States and an obscure twenty years of what would appear to be only desultory painting and virtually no recorded exhibitions, O'Shea appears in Pasadena, California, and exhibits a large body of work to high critical praise. Following a brief period of activity in Southern California, the painter settles for the larger part of his personal and artistic life in that almost mythic natural paradise, the area around Carmel. Like La Jolla and Santa Barbara farther south, Carmel (whether it be the town, the Highlands, or other part of a satellite community) had a fairly large share of a certain type of person—upper middle class to quite wealthy. Unlike its southern counterparts, it also became an artist's colony of distinction, attracting painters and graphic artists of a quite consistent aesthetic persuasion who hymned its natural beauty of landscape and seascape. Although several artists achieved a high degree of eminence in the Carmel-Monterey area, few were as revered and few became as one with the spirit of the place as John O'Shea. His Irish verve (and temper), his unquenchable zest for life and good times, his fervent though erratic periods of production were much discussed staples of an isolated, socially gregarious group of artist-bon vivants who partied almost as much as they painted.

O'Shea's style—fluent, vividly colorful, strong yet with a sensitive finesse—fitted both the man and the place. It summarized a technical excellence and a deep dedication to "beauty" that were much needed in this era of California's art history between the straightforward, quite sober realist painting of the later 19th century and the infinite variations on more progressive trends in the mid and later 20th century. O'Shea epitomized a vivacious and powerful approach to local and more exotic scenery which strongly appealed to a generation confused by radical social and economic modifications in life and by uncertainty about aesthetic values in the multiple changes that emanated from Europe after 1900. It is O'Shea's consistency, his integrity of subject and style, that formed the basis of his enthusiastic acceptance by both Northern and Southern Californians of his time.

Pater patriae (genus *Carmelensis*), the artist was the leader of a varied group of painters who essentially subscribed to his values. In retrospect, their high-spirited praise for works that are a far cry from the deliberate distortions and resistance to older, traditional, formal ideas of many of the major artists of Europe, especially Central Europe, may seem slightly innocent. Certainly, O'Shea himself lived long enough to see many of the qualities he had espoused engulfed in a heaving sea of modernism. Curiously, though, there are general precedents for his optimistic, occasionally decorative devotion to a rich palette

3

in the works of the French painters, from the 1870s through the early 20th century. Although O'Shea did not submit to the influence of Galka Scheyer's Blue Four during their many showings in Northern California in the 1920s, as in the Society of Six there is a sense of Fauve intensity and strength of pure color in his works—albeit much modified in his more self-conscious control of compositional ideas. This is not to say, in any way, that John O'Shea was an avid participant in the developments of modern art that emerged with such overwhelming variety after 1945; but he was capable of abstracting his works in the specialized terms of the Carmel School.

John O'Shea represents an animated, freshly humorous life style with a rich component of old-fashioned Irish-American idealism. His lifetime adherence to certain human and painterly values is admirable. He was a fortunate man in almost all ways, particularly in the years after 1914—in his marriage to Mary Shaughnessy, in his numerous attractive, often magnificent residences, in his wide travels under happy circumstances of time and fortune, and his special place in his community. Especially blessed by living in an area of California that was essentially untouched by much of the international and national disillusionment of the 1930s, and earlier, John O'Shea's career was a triumphal procession in a place that understood and admired him and his triumphs.

Joseph Armstrong Baird, Jr.

3. OCEAN THROUGH TREES; POINT LOBOS, CALIFORNIA, cat. no. 170.

4. GRASS AND HILLS, cat. no. 52.

5

"*Even the autumnal beauty of a New England landscape escapes the traditional repose with which many painters have encompassed it. Through the medium of O'Shea's temperament it loses its virginal aloofness . . .*"

Thelma B. Miller, *Carmel Pine Cone*, October 12, 1934.

Ballintaylor to Brooklyn

This book commemorates the one-hundred-tenth anniversary of the birth of John O'Shea in Ballintaylor, Dungarvan, County Waterford, Ireland, and the thirtieth anniversary of his death in Carmel, California. The need for such a book had been felt for some time, for, although his reputation as a painter was established, neither "who" he was nor exactly "what" he painted was known.

By necessity, much of what is presented about John O'Shea's early life is conjecture or, at best, thoughtfully chosen, since few records exist for the years of his birth, early childhood, and adolescence. Even the family's name change from Shea to O'Shea continues to be undocumented, granting that such name changes were not uncommon for individuals or even entire families without the need for official registration.[1]

While a number of biographical sketches have listed his birth year as 1881,[2] and O'Shea himself maintained that he was born on October 24, 1879,[3] only a baptismal certificate has been located.[4] On it, without a birthdate, he is listed as John Shea, his parents as Patrick Shea and Catherine Egan, and the date as October 15, 1876. Based on Roman Catholic religious practice, strict adherence to which was considerably more prevalent at that time than at the present, one must assume that John was baptized only a day, or at most a few days after his birth, in order to remove his soul from Limbo with all possible haste.

His father, "Pad," a farmer, and his mother, "a big strong woman," were also natives of Ballintaylor. John had two brothers and a sister. When Maurice was baptized on August 14, 1878, he was given the surname of Shea, the same as his father's, while on June 27, 1880, when Alice was baptized, her name and that of her father were recorded as O'Shea. John O'Shea's other brother Michael (Mike), for whom a baptismal certificate is not available, "was a tradesman in the area, who would sometimes spend some time with his brother Maurice."[4]

John O'Shea left his modest home in Ballintaylor when he was fourteen years old, and the family house where he was born stood until about 1965[5] (plate 6). The only known blood relative of John O'Shea alive today appears to be John J. Devine, who lives in England. Devine is the son of John's sister Alice, who married Maurice Devine in 1915.

O'Shea's earliest experience in art remains a matter of speculation as well. In 1919, O'Shea was quoted as having studied in Dublin and Cork, Ireland, as a youth,[6] and in a note found in a family Bible after his death, either he or his wife, Molly, had written that he "learned the elements of drawing, designing and painting at school." While O'Shea was in Dublin, one narrative states that he was connected with the Irish Renaissance, but this is not substantiated in any other sources.[7]

O'Shea once wrote that he came to New York at the age of eighteen.[8] It is also said that he came to the United States at the age of fourteen[9] or sixteen.[10] Depending, therefore, on the year of birth which one chooses to accept, and

6

5. AUTUMN REFLECTIONS, cat. no. 4.

6. John O'Shea's birthplace in Ballintaylor. Family home (rear) and stables which fell to ruins in the late 1960s. Photograph courtesy Mrs. John Barry, Ballintaylor.

7

"O'Shea, I understand, once illuminated books, which may account for the brilliant purity of his color schemes."

Antony Anderson, *Los Angeles Times*, September 16, 1917, Part III.

7. BRILLIANT COVE, cat. no. 136.

8. SEASCAPE; SEA CLOUDS, *ca.* 1916, cat. no. 100.

whether or not he came directly to New York, O'Shea arrived in America between 1890 and 1897. He had at that time no known relatives in the United States.[5]

His arrival in America is not documented, neither are his whereabouts nor activities prior to 1908. Comments by John O'Shea in a letter to his sister-in-law, long after the fact, provide intriguing clues to early residences or activities in New York City and vicinity, but cannot be interpreted fully.[11] He wrote about a friend, "Lyn Lucky Reed was a fine musician. He often played at the Studio *when I was* [my italics] on Union Square and also on 23rd Street." A check of *Trow's New York City Directory*,[12] commencing with 1897, lists a John O'Shea, artist, yearly from 1907–08 until 1912–13. For the first four years, his business address is at 32 Union Square East, Room 1216; for the last two at 132 East Twenty-third Street, Room 9. During this period his home address was in Brooklyn, New York; first at 233 Keap (two years), then at 83 South Tenth Street; 36 South Ninth and 56 South Ninth Street. The first four entries list him as John, the last two as John G.[13]

John O'Shea wrote that he "studied with Professor Whittaker, a fellow Irishman, at the Adelphi Academy." No doubt, this teacher was John Barnard Whittaker (1836–1916), the portraitist who taught at that institution in Brooklyn from 1875 until after 1914.[14] In 1934 John told his wife that he had studied at the Adelphi Academy for two years.[15]

In 1954 he wrote that he had "spent a summer in Leonia [New Jersey] years ago at Harry Eaton (?) Studio."[11] Charles Harry Eaton, A.N.A. (1850–1901), was born in Akron, Ohio, painted in New York and died in Leonia. Whether Eaton's "studio" existed after 1901 is not known.

Several sources state that O'Shea was an "artisan-engraver at Tiffany's,"[16] and, in fact, a John O'Shea is listed on an archival roster of employees at Tiffany and Company in New York City as "a temporary typist in the delivery department from November 29, 1911 to January 15, 1912 at a salary of $10 per week."[17] If this John O'Shea was indeed "our" artist, then the slight embellishment of his position at Tiffany's is quite in keeping with John's frequently documented

8

"Irish humor."[18] He may well have suffered his job as a typist by pretending that it was an engraving task!

Of considerable importance is a comment written approximately seven years later by Antony Anderson, long associated with the *Los Angeles Times*: "O'Shea, I understand once illuminated books, which may account for the brilliant purity of his color schemes."[19] This is another indication that O'Shea did more than typing at Tiffany's.

In the early 1920s, when John O'Shea was living in Carmel Highlands, California, he listed not only his residence as Carmel, but also what was then probably a pied-à-terre for him in New York City at 58 West Fifty-seventh Street.[20] This was the address of the Sherwood Studios and it is possible that he lived there immediately before going to Pasadena, California, in 1913, or intermittently before settling permanently in Carmel Highlands.

A study of entries in Mantle Fielding's *Dictionary*[21] indicates that this was the address given by a considerable number of artists residing in New York City in the mid-1920s. The Sherwood Studios was first listed at this site in 1890,[22] but an 1889 photograph depicts "a party at Sherwood Studio";[23] in the photograph, we can identify such well-known artists as Sam Isham, Robert Reid, Harry Watrous, and Willard Metcalf. The Studios existed there probably until 1951 when the property was sold, the building demolished, and the present office building on the site was constructed.[22] Living there, at Sixth Avenue and

9. CARNIVAL, cat. no. 17.

Fifty-seventh Street, O'Shea could conveniently walk to work at Tiffany's at Fifth Avenue and Fifty-seventh Street and also walk to his classes at the Art Students League at 215 West Fifty-seventh Street.

The League's records for the years 1910–20 were destroyed,[24] but since John also stated that he "studied anatomy with George Bridgeman" [sic] for one year[8,15] and the *only* place where George B. Bridgman (1864–1940), instructor, lecturer, and writer, taught was at the Art Students League, from 1898 until 1942,[25] we must assume that O'Shea was his student there.

Finally, concerning schooling, *News Flashes*, a publication of the William Rockhill Nelson Gallery of Art, Atkins Museum of Fine Arts, Kansas City, Missouri, stated in 1937 in connection with an exhibition of works by O'Shea that "he had studied in Paris and New York."[26] We have not been able to substantiate a period of study in France.

The impetus for O'Shea's move from New York to California is not known. Nineteen thirteen was the year of the epochal international art exhibition at New York's Armory. Preparations for this event had been going on for many months. The resulting show, its immediate reception, and its subsequent influence on American art are immeasurable. It is difficult to imagine why any artist living and presumably working in New York City would have left in the spring of 1913. But on surveying O'Shea's work as a whole and in retrospect, it is not difficult to see that his interest lay neither in the old-line styles of those viewed in National Academy exhibitions, nor in those adopted by a new group of painters known as "The Eight" (Arthur B. Davies, 1862–1928; William J. Glackens, 1870–1938; Robert Henri, 1865–1929; Ernest Lawson, 1873–1939; George B. Luks, 1867–1933; Maurice B. Prendergast, 1859–1924; Everett Shinn, 1876–1953; John Sloan, 1871–1951), who had parted ways with their contemporaries and initially showed their distinctly different but still realist works at the Macbeth Galleries in 1908. Nor does there appear to be a noticeable affinity in O'Shea's *œuvre* for the progressive, abstract trends, largely of European origin, which were to be the "stars" of the Armory Show in 1913 and were subsequently to outshine or influence almost all contemporary American art for many years.

Disillusionment with the apparent success of modern European painting was, however, felt and expressed by some of America's foremost painters, most notably Robert Henri, one of "The Eight." In the words of a recent scholar:

> The embarrassment of being replaced as the leader of modern American art by an 'ultra-modern' movement which he did not fully comprehend was just too great.[27]

As we shall attempt to show later, the considerable number of similarities noted between the life and work of Robert Henri and John O'Shea can be seen as more than mere coincidence.

Prosperity on the Pacific

To explain O'Shea's departure from New York, it can be surmised only that his future wife, Molly, may have been the primary attraction elsewhere.

Molly's parents, James Pollock and Fannie Donally Crawford of Terre Haute, Indiana, derived their wealth from iron and steel mills. They had two daughters: Mary Donally, known as Molly, and Emma List.[28] Molly, born November 28, 1885, received her education at Dana Hall Girls School at Wellesley, Massachusetts.[29] In 1906, she married Walter D. Shaughnessy, aged twenty-five, a real-estate solicitor. He was appointed that year, after examination, to the post of Consular Agent at Charleroi, Belgium, and to Consul at Aguascalientes, Mexico, a year later. Shaughnessy resigned his position with the Foreign Service on April 10, 1910,[30] presumably in order to pursue a different career, but was killed in an automobile accident on January 18, 1911, near a silver mine he owned in Utah.[28]

10. TIDE POOLS, RED HILL, *ca.* 1916, cat. no. 211.

11. ROCKS AND SWIRLS, *ca.* 1916, cat. no. 200.

12. COLORFUL SURF, *ca.* 1916, cat. no. 142.

11

The death of her husband brought great sorrow to Molly, and the young widow was in "deep mourning for a year."[28] Molly's grief was compounded by the death of her father in 1912. She received the news while staying at the Southern Hotel in New York City,[28] and it was probably during this period in New York that Shawn (as she called John) and Molly first met—perhaps at a museum or painting exhibition, both of which Molly was fond of visiting.

After her husband's death, Molly's mother spent some of her time in Pasadena, California. Molly and her sister, Emma, visited her there frequently during the years when she lived at 586 Huntington Terrace and 615 North California Street.

Shawn's arrival in Pasadena in March 1913[10] thus coincides with Molly's early visits there, and about three years later, most probably during 1916, they were keeping house together in a studio/residence in Laguna Beach, California,[15,28] while he retained his residence as a "painter" at 157 Oakland Avenue, Pasadena.[31] That they were keeping house is perhaps too idyllic a phrase. It has been recalled that "Uncle John" was not only a terrible housekeeper, but occasionally threw the dirty dishes out the kitchen window[28]—exhibiting the strong temper which was to remain part of his relationship to Molly before and during their subsequent marriage.

There are clear indications that the thirty-seven-year-old O'Shea had been actively painting before his sojourn in Pasadena. The earliest known critique of his work is from California, dated December 7, 1913. From it one could safely assume that he was an artist before he left New York nine months earlier. He is recorded as exhibiting some "eighteen or twenty of his impressionistic pictures of Southern California" at the studio of Kenneth Avery in Pasadena. Antony Anderson, writer and critic for the *Los Angeles Times*, says they were "wonderfully beautiful interpretations of our landscape full of vibratory light and color."[32] (In 1932 Avery's Studio was at 2020 San Pasqual Avenue in Pasadena;[10] its location prior to that date cannot be documented.) During the same

12

month he is noted as showing some twenty paintings in the large auditorium of the Friday Morning Club in Los Angeles.[33] Antony Anderson again comments: "though sorely tempted, I will season my admiration and write in the soberest prose."[34]

Further, a review of a later exhibition of his works in New York City in 1921, although not mentioning a previous residence in that city, indicates that John O'Shea was painting in Maine before he went to California—scenes from both coasts and a variety of subjects were exhibited.[35]

John O'Shea showed a predilection early in his career for subjects of the sea. Coasts, rocks, waves, coves, and various forms of their interplay were the subjects of works in Maine and along the Southern California coast. Later he would put on canvas and paper many scenes of the ocean near the Monterey Peninsula and islands in the Pacific Ocean.

However, in Maine and on Monhegan Island off the coast of Maine, O'Shea, like many artists before him, fell under the spell of "its rock and surf scenery."[36] He painted not only the coast, but the countryside as well in such works as *October* and *November*—"boldly, broadly and with unabashed color worthy of this most famous of our [Maine] spectacles"[35]—meaning, of course, the fall colors of vegetation on land. A surprising coincidence was noted recently in this regard. Robert Henri was also painting land and sea subjects then, possibly at the same time and place as O'Shea. Henri went to Monhegan Island in the summer of 1911, and while there painted *Surf and Rocks*—in which the elements of painting are reduced to near-abstract shapes, no doubt in order to capture effects of a fleeting moment—and also *Cathedral Woods, Monhegan Island*, a picture of the dense, virgin forest on the island.[37] Somehow related in time and style is O'Shea's stunning *Cove at Sunset* (plate 13), which bears a cryptic inscription on the reverse, "A. Lenique, 1911,"[38] although the locale depicted does not appear to be Monhegan.

Soon after, in California, he was painting land subjects such as "*Revelry,* a lone eucalyptus dancing with the elements . . . in fine expansive sky."[39] (This painting, illustrated in the *Graphic*, was recently rediscovered, going by the title *Eucalyptus Trees in Storm*. It is the earliest known positively documented work of John O'Shea. See plate 1.) The same review article in *Graphic* yields a rare chance to read O'Shea's comments on painting in California:

> One sees California best from eminences where one can view things from a great distance. Foothills, mountains and canyons one can see anywhere—you paint them yellow, drab or seered as they occur, with little accents of spots of oak, but from the high places where I see California it requires a tonal vocabulary to express its vastness and immensity. People go about in motors, and travel over well-beaten roads. They view a line of eucalypti or other picturesque growths and believe they have seen California. After the day's outing there is absolutely no memory left worth while. To see California one must trudge it along in the most primitive fashion. I have lived so intimately with nature since I have been here that were I to go east the impressions I have gathered would remain imperishable and influence all my future work. It is California's ever-changing mood I love best. One cannot reduce these to a formula. I forget that I know anything about paint—and am affected purely by the spirit and beauty of the scene—and when I feel that way my technique becomes subjective.

Finally, as if the specter of Henri, fellow New Yorker and leading artist, should appear in California, on the same page of the article Beatric de Lack Krombach extols the merits of twenty-six canvases by George Bellows, N.A. (1882–1925), being exhibited in the Los Angeles Museum Art Gallery in February 1915. Bellows and Henri and their wives were good friends, and Bellows taught many of Henri's students.[40] Surely O'Shea must have seen Bellows's exhibition, or, at least, been curious about it—he saved the entire page from *Graphic*.

Although some curiosity concerning O'Shea's precipitate departure from New York City in 1913 has been noted, it must be added now that O'Shea had not exactly relocated in an artistic vacuum. South of Pasadena, in Balboa Park at San Diego, preparations were being made for the extensive Panama-California Exhibition which was to open in 1915 and would feature, among other works, paintings by "Robert Henri and his circle of fellow artists, the avantgarde of the day."[41] Incidentally, Henri and his former student, Alice Klauber, were the primary movers for this landmark exhibition in Southern California. To the north, San Francisco was completing arrangements to host the Panama-Pacific International Exposition, lasting from February 20 through December 4, 1915, and extended into 1916 as the "Post-Exposition." In all, over 11,000 paintings, drawings, etchings, and sculpture from all over the world and the United States[42] would be shown at the Marina in San Francisco.

The art colony at Laguna Beach was growing rapidly in 1916 when Shawn and Molly moved there. In her words, it was long before that place was "discovered."[15] By 1917, thirty or forty artists were residing in the village. This was prior to the formation of the Laguna Beach Art Association in 1918, founded largely through the efforts of Edgar Payne (1882–1947).[41]

There exists a caricature of O'Shea, dated 1914, by Malcolm St. Clair, the son of Norman St. Clair (1863–1912), the first artist to paint at Laguna. It is tempting to think that the St. Clairs, who lived in Pasadena (Norman died there in 1912), were known to O'Shea and that Norman's work influenced O'Shea's. In fact, there is considerable similarity in technique between the watercolors of Norman St. Clair and O'Shea from this period, particularly in the application of pigment. Both artists worked in "dry" dots and distinct patches rather than long strokes and "wet" confluent patterns.[43]

Additional and marked similarity is noted between these watercolors and some by Maurice Prendergast, dating from 1910 to 1916.[44] Of passing interest, Prendergast, like Robert Henri, one of "The Eight," exhibited in 1915 at San

13. COVE AT SUNSET, cat. no. 30.

14

"I rejoice that at Laguna Beach [1916] he essayed the watercolor medium, for the clarity of his colors, joined to the jewel-like placement of them, shows him to be triumphantly at his ease in aquarelle."

Antony Anderson, *Los Angeles Times*, September 16, 1917, Part III.

14. COVE AND BATHERS, *ca.* 1916, Coll. The Fieldstone Company, cat. no. 143.

15. GREEN COVE, RED SLOPE, *ca.* 1916, cat. no. 158.

16. VEILED MOUNTAIN, *ca.* 1915, cat. no. 124.

15

Diego on Henri's invitation, as well as at the San Francisco Exposition, being, of course, already well known through innumerable exhibitions in the East.

Of the few paintings known today executed by O'Shea during this time, at least five watercolors correspond to the Pasadena–Laguna Beach period, 1913–17. Almost certainly *Cove and Bathers* and *Green Cove, Red Slope* (plates 14, 15) are views of Fisherman's Cove, near Laguna Beach. Or, less likely, they might be views of Heisler Park Beach.[45] Fisherman's Cove was also depicted by Guy Rose (1867–1925), who painted in Laguna Beach in 1914 after his return from Giverny by way of Narraganset Pier. Rose, incidentally, spent the summers of 1918–20 in Carmel, California,[46] and also lived in Pasadena, where he died

17. COASTLANDS, anonymous collector, cat. no. 24.

Opposite page, VEILED MOUNTAIN, detail of plate 16.

in 1925. A number of other interesting paintings whose whereabouts remain unknown today, but which were described in some detail by Antony Anderson during that era, attest to O'Shea's continuing interest in subjects on land as well as along the coast.

Describing works on exhibition at the Arcade of the Hotel Green in Pasadena, March 1914, Antony Anderson first deplored the fact that John O'Shea had not seen fit to name the twenty or twenty-five canvases because "worded titles are often obscuring and misleading" but then went on to give us these tantalizing descriptions of O'Shea's works:

- those three figures standing on a quay above the sea, all in blues, green and tawny grayish pinks
- colorful canvas showing us the effects of a driving rain on a grove of trees
- the seared hills with rounded contours under a vivid summer sun
- the newly-cut road through hills near Pasadena as bizarre and sparkling as an Italian vista
- the panorama of desert hills under a vast sky and the little lyrics of springtime that many of the smaller pictures are[47]

In December 1914, as a member of the California Art Club, O'Shea joined other artists in an exhibition and sale of paintings at the Blanchard Art Gallery in Los Angeles to benefit a war-relief fund for European artists.[48]

In 1915, Antony Anderson welcomed O'Shea's titles for his second exhibition at the Friday Morning Club and acknowledged a certain humor in them. This latter critique offered titles *and* brief descriptions of a goodly number of early works.[47]

Where Is Carmel Highlands?

18

Opposite page, MARINE-POINT LOBOS, detail of plate 19.

18. SAND KING, cat. no. 202.

O'Shea moved from Southern California to Carmel Highlands between 1916 and 1917. Even after he left, O'Shea maintained professional ties in Southern California, showing works at the Los Angeles County Museum's Summer Exhibitions in 1919, 1920, and 1921.[10] Of passing interest is the fact that all of the paintings shown—a total of five—were lent by a Miss Augusta Senter, whose connection with O'Shea remains unknown otherwise.[49] O'Shea himself would return to Pasadena with a large exhibition of works in the spring of 1928.

John O'Shea's motive for moving to the Monterey Peninsula is not known. Then, as now, many artists visited Carmel, often returning for specific holidays over many years. One visitor to Carmel during the summer of 1917 was George Bellows, N.A., from New York. He was a friend of both Robert Henri and of the painter William Frederick Ritschel, N.A. (1864–1949), of Carmel. Bellows took the "Cooke residence" in the middle of June and stayed for four months.[50]

The earliest recorded appearance of a John O'Shea on the Monterey Peninsula was on October 27, 1916; he was "from Los Angeles, visiting in Carmel, having just arrived at the El Monte Verde."[51] In November 1917, a month after Bellows left, O'Shea arrived at La Playa Hotel in Carmel[52] and now listed his domicile as New York. La Playa was the famous hostelry to-be, developing at that time from the studio of Chris Jörgensen (1860–1935), the artist who had sold the structure consisting of four bedrooms, a bath, and kitchen to Agnes D. Signor in 1913.[53] When Signor died ten years later, business ceased in Carmel for the day in tribute to her.[54]

Although John had lived with Molly in Southern California and was to marry her in 1922, neither his first residence—other than El Monte Verde or La Playa—nor her earliest arrival in Carmel are recorded. John O'Shea, however, was drawn early on to Carmel Highlands.

The whole of what was to become the fashionable Carmel Highlands was then still a relatively "far-away" and uninhabited area. In 1916–17 roads and paths were being cut; by January 1917, "mechanics are working daily on the hotel";[55] in May "construction of a home" began.[56] In March one spoke of "outings to Carmel Highlands" from Carmel;[57] in April visitors were still asking local residents, "where is Carmel Highlands?"[58]

By June El Nido Tea Room had opened at the Highlands Inn,[59] and the first guests were welcomed to the Inn on July 28, 1917.[60] Fare on the Carmel-to-Highlands Stage was twenty-five cents and a special dinner served on Christmas Day was one dollar per plate.[61] John O'Shea arrived in time for "the season" and was among the festive throngs in attendance at "A Long-to-be Remembered Social Affair," a party on New Year's Day, 1918, for members of the Carmel Arts and Crafts Club and friends.

> It is no exaggeration to aver that the most brilliant gathering, intellectually and socially, that has ever assembled on the Monterey Peninsula, was that which was dined and entertained at Carmel Highlands Inn on New Years Day.[62]

19

19. MARINE-POINT LOBOS, cat. no. 69.

20. BLUE PACIFIC, anonymous collector, cat. no. 12.

21. SEA POOL, Coll. John and Lorna Meyer, cat. no. 97.

But O'Shea was not just socializing in his new surroundings. At year's end 1917–18, he had joined thirteen other artists in the winter exhibition of fifty or more paintings in the Hall of the Arts and Crafts Club. "Some of the best pictures are by those who are showing here for the first time."[63]

We surmise that the presence of John O'Shea at Carmel Highlands was somehow related to that of Mrs. Charles Bigelow (Elizabeth T.), art patron, collector of paintings, and wealthy Santa Barbaran.[64] Mr. and Mrs. Bigelow were guests of Mrs. Alice R. Comins, a painter herself, over the holidays 1917–18.[65] Presumably widowed thereafter, Elizabeth Bigelow was deeded property in Carmel Highlands in fall 1918 and spring 1919 by Alice Comins[66] and occupied her new home near the Highlands Inn (today, next door to the Tickle Pink Motor Inn) for the winter season 1919–20.[67] None other than John O'Shea "superintended the building of the Bigelow house, one of the showplaces of the Highlands,"[68] where he subsequently lived for some time.[64]

John established a reputation as "a most eligible bachelor" and became a popular figure in the art community as well as among the literati. He was

20

21

"*He painted the sea many times and he paints it like a man who is not afraid of it. His rocky coasts and hills with cypress trees are all vigorously handled and they carry well too.*"

The New York Herald, November 27, 1921.

22. CYPRESS TREES, cat. no. 32.

23. COAST PINES-HIGHLANDS, cat. no. 22.

24. SEA BEYOND THE ROCKS, Coll. Molly Jeppson, cat. no. 96.

spending a lot of time with another Highlands widow, Alycia H. Clark (Mrs. Wellington Clark?),[64] who sold her home in Hollywood and came to "reside permanently in [a] beautiful home."[69] The likely conclusion that either party was taking advantage of the other, however, would seem unfair. An interesting déjà vu is noted in a witty commentary by Mahonri Sharp Young regarding the painter Paul Dougherty, N.A. (1877–1947), who, when not traveling, was then living in New York City. About 1916, Dougherty, whose second wife had left him, married a lady named Marian Clark. Young wrote in a recent "retrospective" tribute: "Paul did not mourn very long or very much, because he was much in demand around town. He liked the company of rich and attractive women, and they liked his."[70] Dougherty, incidentally, would settle in Carmel Highlands years later with his fourth wife, Paula Gates.

Carmel—At Work and Play (1925), a collection of anecdotes, gossip, and "flowery and evocative descriptions of old Carmel," harking back as early as 1917, introduces O'Shea as having represented the "Highland Colony" painters, along with William Frederick Ritschel, William Clothier Watts (1869–1961), Thomas Shrewsbury Parkhurst (1853–1923), George J. Koch (active in Carmel 1915–40), and Theodore Morrow Criley (1880–1930). The Crileys were building a house[71] at "The Three Corners" in Carmel Highlands in 1917. O'Shea and Criley would later become neighbors, best friends, and steady painting companions.[64,72]

That O'Shea early on had plans to remain in the area is surmised from a quotation, in 1952, that he had come to that part of the country thirty-five years earlier and had been a "diligent gardener since 1917 when he planted the magnificent trees on his Carmel Highlands estate."[73] Actually, "the estate" on which he and Molly built a house was to come somewhat later, in 1924. Also, what might have been meant in this particular interview could have been the cypresses which John planted, according to his friend, poetess Ella Young,[74] on cliff acreage the O'Sheas owned by the ocean, on the south side of Wild Creek Canyon.

Perhaps it was Molly who led the way to Carmel Highlands. A notice following their 1922 marriage in New York City included a statement that Molly owned "a lovely site at Carmel-by-the-Sea," and that "it is probable that they will build a home on this spot"[75] on their return from a European honeymoon. Another stated that Molly "still owns ten acres of property down near Smuggler's [sic] Cove where she expects to build in the near future."[76] Recalling that Molly's first husband had gone to public school in Belmont, California, a community south of San Francisco, and to business college in San Francisco, and that he was a real-estate solicitor in 1905,[77] it seems quite within reason that Walter Shaughnessy or Mr. and Mrs. Shaughnessy purchased real estate in or near Carmel at that time. Perhaps Shaughnessy, like poet George Sterling (1868–1926), the first of many luminaries to reside in Carmel, "came down to Carmel from the San Francisco Bay region with plans and the money to build a house . . . on the last day of a sunny June in 1905."[78] This seems to be one

25

25. OPALESCENT COAST, cat. no. 173.

26. DOWN THE COAST, cat. no. 37.

of two plausible reasons why a young and rather recent widow from Terre Haute, Indiana, who had during married life lived mostly abroad, subsequently met a new beau in New York City and was last living with him in Laguna Beach, California, would suddenly decide to do something with her property in Carmel-by-the-Sea, or more accurately, Carmel Highlands. She owned it! The second possibility could be that Shawn and Molly learned about the new Carmel Highlands area or property while in Pasadena or Laguna Beach, that he went on ahead, and that she came up from Pasadena to visit him, fell in love with the area, purchased property, and decided to marry O'Shea. Records of when she purchased the property have not been located. To date the only property transaction uncovered is the purchase in 1924 by "John O'Shea et ux," of approximately two acres where they built their first house.[79]

On the Monterey Peninsula, O'Shea could not help but be impressed with the exhilarating coastal and marine vistas; many other marine artists have been drawn there as well. John O'Shea thus came in close contact with three important Monterey Peninsula marine painters. In addition to William Frederick Ritschel, these were Paul Dougherty and Armin Carl Hansen (1886–1957). Arthur Hill Gilbert (1894–1970), also an early painter and exhibitor at Laguna Beach,[80] known primarily for his landscapes and portrayal of oak trees, would move there a little later and paint views of the coast near Monterey.

Most likely, these artists were drawn independently, within twenty years or so of each other, to the young art colonies then forming on the Peninsula. Ritschel came about 1909 (or 1911), Hansen in 1913, O'Shea in 1916 or 1917, Gilbert in 1926 or 1928, and Paul Dougherty, a summer visitor as early as 1928[81] and with "headquarters" after 1932.[82] It is said of another artist, Frank Harmon Myers (1899–1956), a younger, well-known portraitist and landscape painter, that his "reputation broadened as he commenced painting the sea in the late 1930s followed closely by his move to the Monterey Peninsula."[83]

Of these six artists, the three most consistent painters of the coast of Monterey were elected to the National Academy of Design for their fine depictions of the sea. Paul Dougherty became an Associate in 1906 and an Academician in 1907 for Atlantic marines; both William Ritschel, Associate in 1910, Academician in 1914, and Armin Hansen, Associate in 1926, Academician in

27

1948, were honored for their work on the Pacific. Arthur Hill Gilbert, a landscapist primarily, but who painted marines as well, was elected an Associate in 1930.[84]

Some indication of the extent to which the Academy *and* the public continued to esteem not only coastal paintings by these artists, but the artists themselves, is a poem printed in 1938:

> The Gall'rys giving another show
> With the same old art that we all know
> And taking the pack of artists in tow
> are
>   The Hansen, The Ritschel
>   and The Great O'Shea.
> There's Midway Point and the Cypress Trees
> And Carmel's Beach whipped by a breeze
> And dotting the walls, thick as fleas
> are
>   The Hansen, The Ritschel
>   and The Great O'Shea.
> The other artists haven't a chance
> Their stuff is passed with never a glance
> They can't survive the concerted advance
> of
>   The Hansen, The Ritschel
>   and The Great O'Shea.
> Along with the wave of the "building boom"
> A new wing of the Gallery is opening soon
> But it will simply provide more room
> for
>   The Hansen, The Ritschel
>   and The Great O'Shea.
>   —Robert S. Vance

(The editors noted: "For what it is worth and absolutely without malice, we publish the following verse, knowing that the gentlemen in question will laugh longest and loudest.")[85]

As it concerns O'Shea, this praise, as we shall see, was probably being applied to other subjects which he painted well, aside from seascapes.

Another reflection of the popularity of paintings of the sea might well be the frequency with which those who painted them were chosen for elective positions in art circles. The Carmel Art Association, the West's oldest art cooperative (founded in 1927), chose as its first three presidents after incorporation in 1934, Armin Hansen, 1934–1937, John O'Shea, 1937–1940, and Paul Dougherty, 1940. O'Shea had been president immediately prior to incorporation as well. Frank Myers was given this honor later, in 1953.[86]

Although John "lingered along the Monterey coast,"[87] he lost no time in establishing an exhibition schedule. He showed two works in the spring of 1918 at the San Francisco Art Association's Annual Exhibition of Contemporary Artists. One of these works, probably the *Ebon Reefs*, was very appealing to a critic who apparently also knew of O'Shea's watercolors.[88] The Oakland Art Gallery, then directed by Worth Ryder (1884–1960), was planning an exhibition of watercolors. The enthusiastic critic wrote, "a charming little marine oil canvas at the Spring Exhibition reminded reviewer of Charles Woodbury" (Charles Herbert Woodbury, 1864–1940, the acclaimed East Coast marine painter) "and was good credential for a watercolor exhibit" of O'Shea's work. Neither the exhibition planned by Ryder nor the one suggested by the critic apparently took place. Ryder was replaced in 1918 by sculptor Finn Haakon Frolich (1868–1947), well known in Carmel Art Circles,[89] and he was succeeded in the same year by William Henry Clapp (1879–1954).[90] To our knowledge, John O'Shea did not exhibit in Oakland until 1933 at the Annual Exhibition of the Works of

27. LOW TIDE, MOUTH CARMEL RIVER, cat. no. 63.

28. HIDEAWAY, *ca.* 1921, cat. no. 55.

29. BLUE SEA, *ca.* 1919, anonymous collector, cat. no. 14.

Western Artists, a yearly event initiated by Clapp, and then it would not be a seascape but one of his now-famous still lifes of bananas.

By March 1919 John O'Shea was ready for his first one-man exhibition in San Francisco. A checklist gave the names of the twenty-two works to be shown at the Helgesen Gallery,[91] one of San Francisco's leading galleries of the day.[92] Anna Cora Winchell of the *San Francisco Chronicle* wrote that O'Shea:

> has been in California about 5 years observing and absorbing our atmosphere and paintable features . . . and will display about 25 oils descriptive of landscape and marine views.[87]

One of the paintings exhibited, *The Blue Sea*, so identified on the reverse, is known today (plate 29). In June O'Shea was showing at the Arts and Crafts Club's Annual Exhibition in Carmel. The brief notice was entitled: "Art Lovers Delighted."[93]

In September 1919 Mr. and Mrs. Thomas Moran from New York registered at La Playa. One cannot doubt that he was accorded as much reverence then as he would be today—"painting as ever at eighty-three."[94]

John O'Shea was mentioned a number of times in society notices after his arrival in Carmel on November 26, 1917, but there was no mention of Molly, although both were said to have been *former* residents of the Highlands when they married in New York City in 1922.[95] For instance, John O'Shea (alone) attends "a most enjoyable dance" at the Highlands Inn in June 1920 with Mr. and Mrs. Theodore M. Criley among other guests.[96] A Mrs. G. S.—not W. D.—Shaughnessy was listed as arriving in Carmel from San Francisco on July 10, 1919. Whether this was a misprint cannot be determined.[97]

Unfortunately, very few of O'Shea's paintings are dated. Judging from subject matter, known whereabouts at certain times, and allowing for stylistic considerations—granting that these may or may not change—one arrives at general time periods for his work. Also helpful are exhibition catalogues or checklists. The few extant photographs and documents sometimes offer clues in dating paintings. In addition, some known critical reviews offer unequivocal

30

31

30. Artist Ferdinand Burgdorff with CORSAIR, by John O'Shea, in patio of Elizabeth Bigelow's house in Carmel Highlands, 1920–21.

31. CORSAIR, *ca.* 1921, cat. no. 28.

32. "Grandma" with John O'Shea, William Ritschel, and, possibly, Belle Zora Ritschel (left to right) photographed *ca.* 1921, near the Highlands Inn. Bird Island and Pt. Lobos, in the distance to the north.

33. GRANDMA, *ca.* 1921, cat. no. 51.

proof of the time that certain works existed. There exist one or more photographic prints of paintings by each of the following photographic studios or individuals: Juley, New York; Lewis Josselyn, Carmel; John Douglas Short, Carmel; Edward Weston, Carmel; and Ansel Adams, San Francisco.

An example of the use of these various methods to place works in their proper chronology is shown by the work entitled the *Corsair*, an oil painting on canvas known today (plate 31). A painting so titled is listed in the brochure for a one-man exhibition of twenty-seven or twenty-eight paintings at the Kingore Galleries in New York City, November to December 1921.[98] On a small snapshot the same painting is seen being displayed by the painter and longtime Peninsula resident, Ferdinand Burgdorff (1881–1975), on what appears to be a stone wall (plate 30). It is, in fact, the stone patio of Elizabeth Bigelow's house described earlier. The setting is remembered well by Richard Criley,[64] for it was at her home that John O'Shea had built young Criley "an imaginative model boat on which he placed some brass plumbing fixtures to look like capstans and other maritime fittings," and Criley sailed it in her pool. The *Corsair* was most likely painted, therefore, sometime between 1919 or 1920, after Bigelow's house was built, and 1921, when it was exhibited in New York. Interestingly, however, in scrutinizing the area around the signature at lower left, as well as cliffs on the center left, and the horizon, it is apparent that additional work was done on it *after* the signature was applied.

The following example signals another era and a different subject matter for John to paint. Although he himself documented having studied prior to 1913 with the portraitist Whittaker and the anatomist Bridgman, it was not until 1921 at the Kingore Galleries that John O'Shea displayed examples of portraiture. The large canvas in somber colors on dark background entitled *Grandma* (plate 33) is reminiscent of a number of similarly posed portraits by artists of the period, all inspired in one way or another, no doubt, by the famous *Study in Black and Gray (The Artist's Mother)*, 1872, by James Abbott McNeill Whistler (1834–1903). O'Shea's painting represents a sitter, whose identity is not yet definitely known, but with whom he was photographed, along with a

33

bearded man and a stylish woman (plate 32), on an elevated, rock-walled terrace overlooking the ocean and Bird Island in Carmel Highlands about 1920. It was originally thought that the scene was taken from the stone mansion being built as a summer retreat during 1917–22 by famed architect Charles Sumner Greene for the family of "D. L." James of Kansas City. "D. L.'s" wealth derived from a crockery wholesale business.[99] He and his wife, Lily, enthusiastically followed the building of their showplace, later named "Seaward."[64] In May 1919, after the foundation for the house was laid and ground work had begun, they were expected to arrive from Kansas City "to watch the pile grow."[100] "D. L." and Lily became good friends of the O'Sheas.

However, a recent visit with Daniel (Dan) James, son of "D. L.," led to the discovery that the picture was really taken from one of the old stone terraces on the Highlands Inn premises across the highway and to the south. The bearded gentleman in the picture is William Ritschel; and while the stylish lady on the right remains unidentified, she may have been the second Mrs. Ritschel, Belle Zora, to whom he was married from 1917 until 1930,[101] but who was rarely at the Highlands. Ritschel lived only a short distance away, down the hill, across the road and at the ocean in his "Castle," built in 1918.[102] This edifice was jovially termed by his friends the "calabozo" (Spanish for prison) because of its relatively primitive amenities and its fortress-like appearance.[64]

Although the recent meeting with Dan James in search of *Grandma's* identity was arranged some months before, it took place, quite inadvertently, during the week that Dan James's identity as "Danny Santiago," author of *Famous All Over Town*, was exposed. That week reporters were furtively seeking details of this intriguing exposé, and it seemed strange to Dan James that we had come only to identify the location and the subjects in an old

34. SILVER CYPRESS, ca. 1934, Coll. Monterey Peninsula Museum of Art, cat. no. 102.

35. NATURAL BRIDGE, ca. 1921, cat. no. 75.

photograph! However, "Danny Santiago" (somewhat loosely the Spanish for Dan James) graciously volunteered perceptive insight into John O'Shea's life and work, if not about the curiously attired *Grandma*. According to James, John O'Shea would have greatly appreciated the story of James taking on the identity of an unknown young Latino author in order to write about the teenage Chato Medina, hero of the story which takes place in the old barrio in East Los Angeles. This book won for the masquerader, James, the prestigious Rosenthal Award for literary achievement in 1984, to the astonishment thereafter of the award committee who, no doubt, had imagined the author to be "an unsophisticated young Latino."[103] (The award is sponsored by the American Academy and Institute of Art.)

The O'Sheas had come to know the Jameses well over the years. At the time when young Dan was becoming politically involved in the longshoremen's dispute in San Francisco, 1933–34, the senior Jameses and the O'Sheas apparently either traveled together to Mexico or met there, as surmised from a

35

"One desert scene is of richly colored rock mountain formations in marked contrast in color with his gray-blue Monterey cypress painting."

H. L. Dungan, *Oakland Tribune,* April 29, 1934.

photograph taken of the foursome in front of what is certainly a pre-Conquest ruin, perhaps when John painted there in 1935 (see plate 117).

While *Grandma* was thought by his heirs to have been O'Shea's mother, Dan James stated emphatically: "John would never have brought his mother to the Highlands; he probably would have kept her in San Francisco!" James doubted whether any of John's relatives from Ireland had ever visited him in the United States. In fact, in closing he said: "John rarely spoke to anybody about his relatives or the Old Sod!"

Obviously this elderly person was someone quite dear to John O'Shea—several photographs were taken of the occasion and the tenderness with which John is holding her by the arm bespeaks affection and closeness. And although he exhibited this portrait of her at Kingore's on Fifth Avenue in New York City, it was "not for sale." A final puzzle presents itself in comparing a studio photo of an earlier version of the painting with the work today; in the final version a painting has been added to the wall above and to the left of "Grandma."

Interestingly, a work that *was* sold at the Kingore exhibit was entitled *The Madrone* (a shrub native to British Columbia found in various parts of California). In all probability it is the oil painting by that name depicting "a landscape with red trees," owned today by the Mills College Art Gallery in Oakland, California; the painting was acquired in 1925, the year the gallery opened.[104]

Both *Grandma* and his most famous portrait, that of friend and fellow artist George Overbury ("Pop") Hart (1868–1933) painted a year later in 1922, were originally executed on a dark background, in a manner resembling certain works of Diego Velásquez or Edouard Manet, and except for a top hat in the Hart portrait, without any distracting trappings to draw the viewer's attention away from the sitter (plate 36). *Pop Hart* was painted at the Sherwood Studios in New York City after John's recovery from a debilitating illness[105] (of unknown origin to us) and prior to his marriage to Molly. It was shown in March 1922 at the Waldorf-Astoria Hotel in the Society of Independent Artists' Annual Exhibition and acclaimed a genuine masterpiece by the very critical Royal Cortissoz of the *New York Tribune*.[106] Interestingly, Cortissoz' admiration singled out O'Shea's work as being among the few notable achievements in the exhibition and worthy of serving as an example of good painting to the other exhibiting artists.

Pop Hart has been shown often since and hangs today at the Bohemian Club in San Francisco. O'Shea presented the painting to the Club following its exhibition there in May 1947 in *75 Years of Bohemian Art*, a show featuring works by artist-members of the Club.[107]

Whether O'Shea exhibited *Pop Hart* and the thirty-odd paintings shown at the Kingore Galleries elsewhere in the East is not known. But a fine arts insurance policy issued to him by United States Lloyds, Inc. of New York on May 31, 1923, presumably for the return shipment of paintings to California, listed only six works. Of these, only *Pop Hart* is known today while five are unlocated. Of those exhibited but not on the policy, *The Madrone* was sold and *Grandma* was also returned at some time. The rest, approximately twenty-six, were perhaps sold, but remain unlocated.

Molly and Shawn obtained a marriage license in New York City on May 25, 1922, and were married three days later at John's residence, 58 West Fifty-seventh Street (The Sherwood Studios). Molly had been staying a few doors away at the Great Northern Hotel on West Fifty-seventh Street (see plate 178), possibly with the witnesses to her betrothal, Mr. and Mrs. Benjamin H. Pine (Molly's sister Emma and her husband), and their daughter Mary Frances. O'Shea gave his age as forty-two and she as thirty-six.[108] Patrick J. Grattan Mythen, Archabbot in the Eastern Orthodox Catholic Church, St. Nicholas

36. PORTRAIT OF "POP" HART, 1922, Coll. Bohemian Club, San Francisco, cat. no. 90. Photograph by Juley, New York, *ca.* 1922.

37 and 38. John and Molly O'Shea, *ca.* 1922. Photographs by Arnold Genthe, New York.

37

38

Cathedral, solemnized the rites of matrimony. In addition to the ordinary certificate, Archabbot Mythen, thinking it "would be rather a joke to you with your artistic sense," sent a colorful "Russian Manuscript" to John.[109]

Its letterhead reads:

THE ARCHDIOCESE OF THE ALEUTIAN ISLES AND NORTH-AMERICA

OF THE HOLY EASTERN ORTHODOX-CATHOLIC CHURCH

UNDER THE JURISDICTION OF

HIS HOLINESS, THE PATRIARCH OF MOSCOW AND ALL RUSSIA

On the Marriage Certificate John O'Shea listed himself as a "Citizen of Irish Free State." On May 31 he was issued a British Passport, documented by the United Kingdom of Great Britain and Ireland, as a "British Subject by birth."[110]

A beautiful studio portrait of Molly and an equally handsome one of John were made by photographer Arnold Genthe (1869–1942) in New York City— probably at this time. Genthe knew California well, especially San Francisco, where he began his productive career in 1897,[111] and Carmel, where he built a house and lived for about ten years. He moved to New York City in 1911.[112]

Other than a brief mention in various sources of the O'Sheas' "wide travels" in Europe during their honeymoon and of John's "frequent" visits there, we

39

have no known documentation to trace these itineraries. There were inferences and allusions at different times[113] to their travels in Ireland, southern Europe, "sunny Normandy," Inland (Europe), Paris, Africa, and Alaska. "Artist John O'Shea and his bride are visiting Mr. O'Shea's mother in Ireland" proclaimed an item in "Purely Personal Paragraphs" of the *Carmel Pine Cone*, August 31, 1922, but an in-law of John O'Shea living today in Ballintaylor wrote recently that John never visited there after he left home, nor did any of his Irish relatives, in turn, visit him in the United States.[5] This would affirm the statement by Dan James mentioned above. The only evidence to indicate a European trip is a pair of crayon drawings, almost duplicate studies, of gnarled and entwined trees resembling a man and woman in amorous embrace, one of which bears the inscription "Olive Trees—Majorca" and is signed John O'Shea, perhaps painted on that Spanish Island in the Mediterranean (plate 39). Ample evidence, of course, does exist of later travels in the United States, Mexico, and the Pacific. "After a long absence in the East and abroad, John O'Shea and his wife have returned. They will be located at Carmel Highlands for several months" said the *Carmel Pine Cone*, June 2, 1923.

A remarkable story, differing in many ways from the preceding account of John O'Shea's arrival in the United States and his honeymoon in Europe, was recently told by his nephew, John J. Devine of Chelsea, London, England. It may also reveal the identity of *Grandma*! Devine wrote in his first letter[9] that O'Shea had attended "an ordinary school in Ballintaylor," had never gone to Cork or Dublin and had left home at the age of fourteen for the voyage to America with two sisters, Catherine and Bridget. (These two sisters were previously unmentioned.[4,5] According to John J. Devine, Catherine, being older, had apparently left home before John Devine's mother, Alice, was born.) Catherine eventually married a John Dwyer and settled in Scranton, Pennsylvania; Bridget went on to California, where she died and was buried in Santa barbra [sic]. (A second letter[114] indicated that Bridget had joined Catherine in Scranton and had died there.) Further, according to the first letter, "John married and came as far as Italy on his honeymoon, and was advised to keep out of Ireland owing to the troubled times." In this vein the *Carmel Pine Cone*

39. OLIVE TREES, MAJORCA, NO. 1, cat. no. 249.

40. TOWARD YANKEE POINT, *ca.* 1920, Coll. Molly Jeppson, cat. no. 117.

"They knew that though he has been devoted for a score of years to the wild beauty of the Carmel and Highlands coastline, he has painted it far less frequently than most of the artists resident here!"

Thelma B. Miller, *Carmel Pine Cone*, September 27, 1935.

for March 17, 1923, referred to upheavals in Ireland, in connection with the writings and satires of a well-known Irish woman of letters: "Turbulence in Ireland Halts Not Lady Gregory's Pen."[115] Moreover, regarding *Grandma*, John J. Devine recognized her in a photograph as his Aunt Bridget from Santa Barbra [sic]![114] To our knowledge neither John nor Molly nor anyone else since their death ever mentioned that two of his sisters had lived or were ever living in the United States.[116] However, we are still confronted with two distinctly different stories—one from Ireland, the other from England. The former is from a distant in-law, the latter from a nephew of John O'Shea (and of "Grandma," the sitter in the painting)!

As well as can be ascertained, Molly and Shawn O'Shea lived together at several different locations on the Monterey Peninsula following his initial stay at Elizabeth Bigelow's home. After their return from Europe in 1923[117] they rented a home for a few months in the Highlands below the Crileys'[64] near "Criley's Beach"[118] and Bird Island. Next, before going to Pasadena for the winter of 1923–24 they were "sojourning in Pebble Beach."[119] By April 1924[120]

41

42

they had returned, but where they lived while their new house was being built farther south on property purchased in June 1924[79] is not known. The house in progress was on a slope overlooking the ocean near the ridge which forms Yankee Point (plate 42). In retrospect we believe that this was part of the ten-acre property mentioned earlier and said to be "down near Smuggler's [sic] Cove." It would include contiguous cliff acreage on today's Spindrift Road along the shore, land across Spindrift Road south toward the site where the house was built, and a small studio building on land across the highway (not completed until 1937) and up the hill and to the west side of Lower Walden Road (plate 41). The couple spent much time designing, furnishing, and decorating this house, occupied most likely during 1924.[121] John was continuously enlarging plans and designing special features such as wooden handcrafted door knobs.[64] That "additions were being built on the O'Shea residence" in Carmel Highlands rated a comment in the *Carmel Pine Cone*.[122] O'Shea planted trees, gardened, built stone walls and paths—hobbies which he enjoyed throughout life.[123] However, expenses of the original house "ran up the cost to the point that their resources never stretched to go ahead with the final home" which they had intended to build![64] They named their residence "Tynalacan."[124] Today it is the "Villa Highland" (Box 232), adjacent to and west of the Carmel–San Simeon Highway (now Highway 1).[125]

About 1938 they sold "Tynalacan" and rented a house in Pebble Beach across the street from "The Witch Cypress" on Seventeen Mile Drive, which runs along the coast (see plate 140). They were living here when Molly died in 1941. This domicile was followed, 1942–46 or 1947, by one which John probably rented at Wild Cat Canyon in the Highlands, the cliffside home of producer Richard L. ("Rick") Masten (see plate 153). John's last home, from 1946 or 1947 until his death in 1956, was in Carmel Woods at San Carlos and Vista Avenue (see plate 160); today it is the home of artist Frank N. Ashley.[28]

"On about six acres" at the ocean on the south side of Wild Cat Canyon was where Shawn and Molly planned to build their final "dream house" but never did so.[64] Many picnics and beach parties, however, were held at this so-

"At night in that house by the sea that John O'Shea's pictures and Molly's rose damasks and blue enamels made so colourful."

Ella Young, *Flowering Dusk*.

43

41. O'Shea's studio, formerly a dairy building dating from the late 1800s, is now a residence on Lower Walden Road. Photograph, *ca.* 1940, and information courtesy Richard M. Blaney, Carmel.

42. Newly built "Tynalacan," the O'Sheas' house in Carmel Highlands, *ca.* 1925. Building surrounded by trees, upper left, was John O'Shea's studio for many years. Old county road, now highway, runs between buildings in foreground and studio.

43. HIGHLANDS COAST, cat. no. 162.

44. TURQUOISE BAY, cat. no. 215.

45. BROWN PROMONTORY, cat. no. 137.

44

45

called "Cliff Property"—on the sand and on a makeshift terrace on the lofty cliff accessible only by a steep flight of steps carved in the rock.[126]

John kept two studios during his painting career; one was a separate building in the Highlands on Lower Walden, the other was a structure adjacent to their Pebble Beach home. The Lower Walden studio and surrounding property was sold in 1946; both studio buildings still stand.[127] At his last residence in Carmel Woods, O'Shea painted in the living room of his home.[28]

Lastly, Shawn and Molly purchased several acres in the Rio Piedras (Rocky Creek) Reservation. This was a non-profit association especially organized to preserve the natural beauty of the area by preventing it from being "developed"—the fate of much of the coastal property becoming accessible then—in

46

"He does not paint like an academician. The work is imaginative and stirring."
Thelma B. Miller, *Carmel Pine Cone*, October 12, 1934.

the wake of completion of the coast highway. All members of the association had access to this communal property, and privileges included the use of a modest cabin with cooking and some sleeping accommodations.[64] In August 1932 they entertained Charlotte Wilson Arthur[128] there; she was the wife of poet Chester Alan Arthur, President Arthur's grandson, who after deciding to "work for the Irish Cause" renounced his English name "Chester" in favor of the Celtic name "Gavin."[129] The O'Sheas' share of this property was willed to Molly and John Williams, their godchildren and namesakes, children of Theodore Criley's daughter, Cynthia, and Dr. Russell Dudley Williams, married in 1935[130] and now divorced.[64]

Most of these property transactions were handled for the O'Sheas by realtor Seth Ulman. He and his wife, Rose, were friends of Shawn and Molly. Years later, in 1955, Seth died several months before John, but it appeared almost providential to John that Seth was able to dispose of all of John's property to his complete satisfaction just a few days before Seth's death.[131]

Returning to 1922, O'Shea became a member that year of the American Watercolor Society to which he belonged until 1941.[132] He retained an interest

47

48

46. SOUTH COAST, MONTEREY COUNTY, *ca.* 1930, Coll. Mr. and Mrs. Anthony R. White, cat. no. 104. Photograph courtesy Anthony R. White.

47. PORTRAIT; BEARDED MAN, cat. no. 181 (for possible identity, see n. 379).

48. PORTRAIT OF BEARDED MAN, cat. no. 87.

in this medium as well as in oil throughout his career (plates 47, 48). Somewhat later he used graphite and crayon and often combined two or more of these media. Toward the end of his life he also tried his hand at etching.

In 1923, while Shawn and Molly busied themselves buying property and making plans for a new house, John's good friend Theodore Criley and his family were traveling in Europe together with John's former hostess Elizabeth Bigelow.[64,133] William Ritschel was sailing in the South Seas and keeping a diary rich in the visual impressions that only an artist could sense. Fortunately, he was also capable of writing exquisite passages to accompany these sketches, in which he described his reactions to the seemingly endless beauty of nature and his surroundings.[134]

No doubt Ritschel shared his experiences with Shawn and Molly on his return.[135] O'Shea kept a copy of Ritschel's account of "his long cherished dream to visit the mysterious islands of the Tuamotu Archipel [sic]" and "the Marquesas Islands, the most romantic and unexplored islands of the Pacific which has come at last to realization." Ritschel was cognizant, no doubt, of Paul Gauguin's life and work in Polynesia and the Marquesas Islands, cut short by his death there in 1903 at the age of fifty-five. Ritschel, then fifty-nine, was on a voyage full of expectations and anxiety. His description of the event is full of the hardships endured by the seafarers and natives; however, his fascination with this idyllic realm led to later visits in 1924 and 1928–30. Yet it is safe to say

49

50

49. TAHITI SHORES, ca. 1928, Coll. Molly Jeppson, cat. no. 209.

50. William F. Ritschel, ON THE LAGUNE [sic], MOOREA, TAHITI, n.d., oil on wooden panel, 20″ × 24″, Coll. Paul Messer Antiques, Moss Landing, California.

51. LATE AUTUMN, Coll. Anne Dickman-Grant, cat. no. 61. Photograph courtesy Anne Dickman-Grant.

that Ritschel's paintings of the tropics never received the acclaim accorded his mainland marine scenes. The O'Sheas would embark on a long, but perhaps less grueling voyage to the South Pacific in 1928.

Theodore Criley, O'Shea's friend and fellow painter, was another early Highlands resident. Born in Lawrence, Kansas, in 1880, he studied painting at the Chicago Art Institute and was a pupil of Lucien Seymour (no dates) and René Ménard, probably M. A. E. René Ménard (1862–1930) in Paris.[136] Leaving behind a career in the hotel business in Chicago and Kansas City, he moved west in the early teens, built a waterfront home in Carmel Highlands in 1917, which he sold in 1928,[137] but lived nearby until his untimely death in 1930. From the front page obituary in the *Carmel Pine Cone*,[138] one readily perceives that Criley, in addition to his art devotion, was keenly involved in civic activities in Carmel.[139] In 1922, in a slightly different arena, *The New York Times* headlines reported Criley's duel with writer/novelist Harry Leon Wilson. Wilson had objected to Criley's undue, if not fervent, advances in his role as John Sayle, 10th Baron Otford, toward Wilson's wife, Helen, the female lead, Mme. Lucie Lachesnais, during their performance of *Pomander Walk* in an amateur theatrical production at Carmel's Forest Theater.[140] As expected, the younger Criley won "the five rounds of fisticuffs, stripped to the waist, their hands protected by thin riding gloves." Wilson survived, as did his marriage to Helen—for another five years, at least. Helen was his third wife, the beautiful daughter of writer Grace MacGowan Cooke.

John was painting again in 1923. "Pop" Hart, to whom he wrote at his home in Coyoteville, New Jersey, was happy for this and glad that he was "preparing for winter exhibitions."[141] Many days were spent painting with Theodore Criley. In tune with each other's work, but also critical, they discussed its merits at length.[64]

O'Shea showed in September 1924 at the Eighteenth Annual Exhibition of Paintings by Artists of Carmel,[142] and Molly and Shawn spent the holidays over Christmas and New Year's in Pasadena.[143]

The O'Sheas' circle of friends in Carmel Highlands and the surrounding towns grew steadily in the years subsequent to the completion of their house on the ridge near Yankee Point. In addition to the Crileys and "D. L." and Lily

James, they associated with poet Robinson Jeffers and his wife, writer Una Call Kuster. This couple had come to Carmel in 1914, taking George Sterling's place, so to speak, after Sterling was divorced by his beloved Caroline (Carrie) Rand and subsequently left for New York.[144] Lincoln Steffens, "muckraker" *par excellence*, arrived in 1926 with his wife, writer Ella Winters; they were among the founders of *The Carmelite*. Playwright Martin A. Flavin and his wife, Sarah, Ella Young (1879–1956), the poetess who had come from Ireland in 1925, and somewhat later, photographer Edward Weston were also among the O'Sheas' friends.

John O'Shea's friendship with William Ritschel was by necessity a very sporadic one. Ritschel was already residing in the Highlands when John O'Shea first arrived in Carmel in October 1916 for a visit. Ritschel, who was first married in Germany in 1893 and had two children, presumably before coming to the United States,[101] married his second wife Belle Zora in April 1917[145] in Riverside, California. Through the years, however, the second Mrs. Ritschel, who it is said[64] had a severe medical problem, rarely lived at the Highlands, although she did visit there occasionally, attended parties, and sometimes took

52. TREES, cat. no. 119.

53. COAST HILLS, cat. no. 20.

a cottage in Carmel.[146] Mr. Ritschel himself traveled extensively during this time, including long stays in Paris, New York City, Arizona, the Mt. Shasta area, and particularly in Moorea, the "Pearl of the Pacific," where he lived in a bamboo hut.[147] In May 1926, Ritschel again returned from a long journey abroad, this time accompanied by "his fiancée and secretary, Elanora 'Nora' Havel,"[148] whom he eventually married in October 1930 in Reno, Nevada, just hours after being granted a divorce from Belle Zora on grounds of mental cruelty.[149]

There is no doubt that O'Shea respected Ritschel as a man and as a painter, although O'Shea sometimes inadvertently expressed feelings of hostility toward Ritschel. Perhaps this hostility was due to envy because Ritschel had attained status in the National Academy of Design. At parties, for instance, when both "D. L." James and Ritschel were present, John's wit and sharp tongue would lash out in biting sarcasm at Ritschel, but would turn to "D. L." with jocular jousting. John especially found ground to criticize Ritschel's fre-

54

55

quent appearance with the intent to "look like an artist," as well as his outlandish painting garb, consisting of flowing flower-patterned lavalava (Polynesian cotton print wraparound) and ahola (loosely fitting shirt), in which he would sit on the rocks to paint. In later years O'Shea would also grow to resent Nora's brash, unabashed, and sometimes staged salesmanship of her husband's paintings—all too often of the same coastal and marine scenes in seemingly monotonous procession.[64]

Unlike Ritschel, John O'Shea was not a member of the National Academy. Whether by accident, conjecture, or "Freudian slip," however, he was accorded this honor by the local Carmel press at least twice. The first of these came off in 1931 as follows:

> The exhibition [at the Denny-Watrous Gallery] contains 31 canvases by John O'Shea, A.N.A., of Carmel Highlands, whose one man show is his first here in several years. Whether pleased or not, no one can linger without realizing that they are facing something tremendous in the art world.[150]

The second, in tandem almost, but about a different show, reads as follows:

> Five who are exhibiting [Carmel Art Association at Denny-Watrous Gallery] Arthur Hill Gilbert, William Ritschel, Paul Dougherty, Armin Hansen and John O'Shea are members of the National Academy and are widely known for their work throughout the country.[151]

These lines may or may not be related to Thelma B. Miller's later comment (in 1934) which is recorded here on page 46.

It is far beyond the scope of this book to even speculate on the reason why John O'Shea was not elected to the National Academy. To be sure, few artists are—only about half-a-dozen of them lived on the West Coast at that time—and their relative merits as painters are certainly not the only considerations in the recommendation and selection process. Others are surely style-in-vogue, direct or circuitous ties with the Academy or members thereof, and general political affiliations, which may or may not be recognized by the decision-making body prevailing in the Academy at the time. Whether John O'Shea was a good painter *in his time* we can only judge from the expressions offered by a wide selection of contemporary critics and fellow artists, and these were—as we attempt to show—serious, abundantly favorable, and often superlative in their evaluation of O'Shea's art.

54. VIOLENCE, cat. no. 126.

55. TORMENTED SEA, cat. no. 116.

56. RAGING SEA, cat. no. 92.

Desert and Bananas

"'Sunset Butte,' 'Superstition Mountain,' 'Torre de Viento,' 'Apache Stronghold,' 'Prospector's Paradise,' are strong powerful canvases. In their purity of color, we find a direct contradiction to the muddy blacks and murky blues and browns of the most recent Modern School, and still they must be called 'modern.'"

"John O'Shea showing at Beaux Arts Gallery," *The Carmelite*, May 16, 1928.

57. UPLAND SOLITUDE, ca. 1927, cat. no. 122.

Little is known about the O'Sheas' whereabouts during the years from 1925 to 1927. For some unknown reason Molly O'Shea spent three months in New York City in summer of 1925.[152] Most likely on more than one occasion during 1926 and 1927 O'Shea traveled to Arizona to paint.[64] Whether Molly accompanied him on any of these trips is uncertain—she was, however, in Carmel in June 1926 at an Arts and Crafts Tea.[153]

Apparently John O'Shea never painted from photographs. Much of his outdoor work was done on the spot, and he often camped out for longer periods when he was moved to paint.[64] During one of these painting trips, almost certainly in 1926, John spent several months driving from place to place, camping out, and painting with Theodore Criley. Criley built a special carryall for this expedition from a model "T" Ford station wagon. It could accommodate the artists and their painting gear, including new, stretched canvases and finished paintings. Their exact itinerary is not known, but one surmises where they chose to paint on the basis of existing works or titles in subsequent press reviews. Thus we know about *Superstition Mountains*, near Phoenix; *Papago* (Indian Territory); *San Xavier de Bac Mission*, *Patagonia*, and *Canelo Hills*, probably meaning Canille Mountains, south of Tucson. They also visited and painted near Nogales on the Mexican border.[64,154]

John was fond of sketching and would often enlarge upon primary impressions in his studio. In a good many instances, however, the rapid sketches themselves displayed accomplished and deft creations worthy of finished works.[155] John was a spasmodic or sporadic painter—sometimes it is said working in a feverish frenzy and at others ignoring his art.[156] Richard Criley related the following story about the 1926 desert trip. It reflects O'Shea's temperament and zeal when he was inspired to paint:

> On one occasion during this trip John and my father were painting together. It was a very mountainous area, with storm clouds and sun breaking through. My father and John had separated and hiked away looking for subject matter. The weather turned very stormy, with sudden winds and bursts of rain. My father gave up trying to hold his canvas down, packed up his gear and went looking for John. He found him in front of his canvas, painting feverishly and swearing a blue streak. The wind was tossing the canvas, the spurts of rain were coming in bursts, but John wouldn't quit.

This painting's whereabouts is unknown. It was last seen in O'Shea's home in Carmel toward the end of his life.[64]

That John and Theodore did not spend all of the time in the desert that year is surmised from notices of exhibitions of their works, although they may not have attended the events. Oliver's Curios Shop showed works by Criley in June,[157] and a larger, very well-received exhibition of his watercolors and oils, including "a portrait of his son," was presented at Carmel.[158]

In October 1926 during the inaugural celebrations of the San Carlos Hotel

58

59

58. EARLY SPRING, ARIZONA, cat. no. 39.

59. Robert Henri (American, 1865-1929), SUMMER STORM, 1921, oil on canvas, 26⅛″ × 32⅛″ (64.5 × 81.4 cm). Coll. Vassar College Art Gallery, Poughkeepsie, New York, gift of Mr. and Mrs. Charles J. Malmed.

60. GRAND CANYON NO. 2, cat. no. 50.

in Monterey, they each contributed to "the hanging of a very representative group of paintings by well-known artists of the Monterey Peninsula"[159] in the new art gallery at the hotel. Recently, at the 1984 inauguration of the new Monterey Sheraton Hotel on the site of the old San Carlos, works by a good many artists who had originally shown there were exhibited—among them was one of O'Shea's famous still lifes of bananas, as well as two by Theodore Criley, a still life of zinnias and a remarkable portrait of "D. L." James.

Conviction and honor were traits apparently esteemed and upheld with force and vigor by artists O'Shea and Criley. One cannot overlook the possibility that these men resembled each other not only in artistic endeavors, but in personal behavior, ethics, and demeanor. As previously noted, Criley vigorously defended his honor after the Forest Theater debacle; now, in 1926, on his return from Arizona he was called upon to defend his son's. When told that the "bullying superintendent" of the high school had accused his son Richard of stealing from lockers, Theodore Criley drove to the school and elicited a profuse apology from the superintendent, but not before threatening to throw him out of the school's second-story window.

As mentioned earlier, there are also interesting parallels between the life and work of Robert Henri and John O'Shea. The preceding account of the desert incident, narrated by Richard Criley many years after the deaths of both O'Shea and Henri, bears an uncanny resemblance to a passage regarding Henri's painting habits described in *Robert Henri and His Circle*:

> There are several important reasons underlying Henri's impulse to complete his pictures as quickly as possible. In later years, he increasingly came to believe that the work of art represented the imprint of the painter's state of being—an elevated state of functioning of mind and body that occurred only at brief moments in man's existence. Therefore, he tells us: "Paint like a fiend when the idea possesses you." This creative process was chronicled by Mary Fanton Roberts in a rare eye-witness account of Henri painting at Woodstock in 1921. Apropos of *Summer Storm, 1921* (plate 59), she wrote:
>
> > He had been painting quietly in his studio when suddenly a terrific storm roared and flashed up over the top of the mountain

"He is not afraid to paint the sunlight, the strong reds and the delicate rose and ivory of sandstone cliffs, the purple and mauve and unbelievable savage blue of desert mountains; the hardness of stone, the strength of canyon walls, the life in the tree as it thrusts itself out of the soil or clings with strong talons to a rock-cranny."

Impressions of John O'Shea's paintings enclosed in letter from Ella Young to Thomas Carr Howe, Jr., April 27, 1934.

and blew down, wild and sweet, over the hillside. . . . As the fury of the storm broke, he painted like mad the tumbling white and gray clouds, the shadowed valley, the tumult of the wind in the trees. The great volume of the storm seemed to pour through his very spirit and on to the canvas. He appeared a part of this sudden rush of furious power that was sweeping over the earth. For the moment he had withdrawn from the world of people and was immersed in the mighty, terrifying spectacle that nature had flung forth.

A better description would be hard to find; it illustrates how he was caught up in the spirit of the moment—in this case, one of nature's rare moods that moved him deeply. Henri's empathy with the storm suggests a distant ancestry in Turner's seascapes, which likewise resulted from the artist's ability to channel the dynamic forces of nature through his own personality, committing these energies to canvas in freely brushed strokes. Van Gogh, too, must come to mind as one of Henri's sources, though, thus placing the American squarely in the tradition of twentieth-century Expressionism, transplanted to American soil.[160]

61

It is said that Henri's spontaneity in painting derived originally from reading William Morris Hunt's *Talks About Art*.[161] This "was one of the most influential treatises on art in circulation during the late nineteenth century . . . it greatly influenced Henri's teaching."[162]

In mid-October 1927, after the recent organization of the Carmel Art Association,[163] the O'Sheas and the Crileys were among "Throngs Viewing New Paintings by Carmel Artists as New Gallery Opens Doors." These were the new quarters for the Carmel Art Association in the Seven Arts Court.[164]

An apparently novel approach to the sale of art works was initiated by the Messrs. Gensler and Lee, well-known San Francisco merchants and art collectors, who later became known especially as jewelry and watch salesmen. Beginning December 12 and lasting two weeks, these entrepreneurs offered art for sale "on a divided payment plan"—known today variously as budget plan or convenient payment plan. The event was held at the East West Gallery in the Women's Building in San Francisco. Works by O'Shea and other prominent painters and sculptors were offered.[165]

The O'Sheas were at home in Carmel Highlands during year's end 1927–28.[166] Jenny Vennerstrom Cannon, noted art critic and a painter herself, offered a long and thought-provoking article after viewing the New Year's exhibition at the Del Monte Hotel Gallery. Among her comments were:

> One looks in vain for the wild bizarre canvas here. . . . There are, however, the pronounced moderns. The work of John O'Shea and William Clothier Watts are decidedly contemporary.[167]

No doubt Miss Cannon was reflecting on an anticipated brouhaha in Carmel's artistic circles which never materialized. Briefly, Gene Hailey, artist and writer for the *San Francisco Chronicle*, had predicted in the summer of 1926 that:

> Mme. E. E. Scheyer, the exponent of ultra-modern art (through her Blue Four group), has gone to Carmel to prepare lectures and exhibitions that will cause the downfall of the Carmel city walls of culture and erudition.[168]

61. ARIZONA DESERT, cat. no. 3.

62. COLORED MOUNTAINS, *ca.* 1927, cat. no. 25.

This onslaught notwithstanding, Carmel's art community not only enjoyed Mme. Scheyer's lectures, lantern slides and all, but her personal stage delivery as well, and Gene Hailey's predictions quite to the contrary, artistic revolution and the "downfall" of culture failed to materialize.[169] Mme. Scheyer, better known as "Galka" Scheyer, represented "an oracular group of European modern masters who exhibited in the United States as "The Blue Four."[170] They were: Alexej von Jawlensky (1864–1941), Wassily Kandinsky (1866–1944), Lionel Feininger (1871–1956), and Paul Klee (1879–1940).

The O'Sheas left shortly for Pasadena where John would "place several of his pictures on exhibition,"[171] including the showing of *Monterey Coast* at the Exhibition of California Artists at the Pasadena Art Institute in January[172] and in February an extensive collection of his newest works at Grace Nicholson's Treasure House of Oriental Art Gallery (later the Pasadena Art Museum and ultimate recipient of "Galka" Scheyer's Blue Four collection).[173]

"The thirty canvases he has on display constitute a group of works as fine as any ever shown in this city, and the artistry shown in the studies ranks the painter among the best exponents of modern art."

Pasadena Star News, February 7, 1928.

The Arizona painting expedition resulted in a major collection of oil paintings shown during the spring of 1928. Beginning in Pasadena at Grace Nicholson's Galleries at 46 North Los Robles Avenue (February–March), the exhibition moved to Tucson's Temple Art Gallery (March–April). Thereafter, it moved to San Francisco's Beaux Arts Galerie (April–May). Active from 1925 to 1933, this prominent center was created and directed by Beatrice Judd Ryan after she had been persuaded by artists such as Maynard Dixon (1875–1946) "to open a gallery devoted to modern art."[174]

Two additional exhibition sites were indicated at that time, but their actual occurrence could not be substantiated. On May 4, 1928, while the exhibition was still hanging at the Beaux Arts Galerie in San Francisco (until May 21), the *Carmel Pine Cone* reported O'Shea's return from a "triumphant trip in the south where his pictures were such a sensation" and stated that O'Shea "showed his work in New York after San Antonio."

Considering the time schedules for Pasadena, Tucson, and San Francisco (February–May), it would seem unlikely that New York and San Antonio could

63. TAHITIAN SCENE, ca. 1928, cat. no. 111.

64. VILLAGE SCENE, cat. no. 125.

have been fitted in as well. Perhaps, however, *after* San Francisco the exhibition did go to New York as John O'Shea (in San Francisco himself) indicated that it might.[175]

From the *Pasadena Star News* to *Argus*, the aspiring new monthly "Journal of Art Criticism"; from the *Los Angeles Times* to the principal Tucson daily and several San Francisco papers, the praises for John O'Shea's paintings flowed in paragraph after paragraph. Save for a few sour notes, this acclaim was universal in placing O'Shea's work in the forefront of contemporary California art. Writing as if today, Jehanne Biétry Salinger, a grand lady of the arts, ended her brief critique: "The hand that is responsible for these long strokes on these canvases has no repose. Exultant? Yes, this work is, but not co-ordinated, not pulled together."[176]

In early August 1928, Molly and Shawn were guests of the Wattses in their elegant Italian villa, built 1922–23,[177] at Wild Cat Canyon in the Highlands. Painter William Clothier Watts, whose numerous world travels are documented on many canvases and watercolors, was an early visitor to Carmel. A week later, on August 16, 1928, Shawn and Molly were bid farewell by a large party of friends[178] in San Francisco as they embarked aboard the liner *Makura* for a journey to the South Pacific.[179] The new British passport issued to the couple lists permission to visit "French Oceania, Fiji Islands, British Samoa, Tonga, Ellice Islands and the United States of America."[180]

"My thoughts had been on John O'Shea's pictures for quite a long while, ever since I heard he had been to the South Sea Islands and painted demon bananas and magical rose and purple fishes."

Ella Young, *The Carmelite*, March 5, 1930.

From this document it is interesting to learn something about their physical appearances at the time. He was almost forty-nine, five feet nine inches tall; his eyes were brown and his hair greyish-brown. Molly was forty-three years old, five feet six and one-half inches tall and had blue eyes and light-brown hair.

Molly was apparently a good driver and at home often drove the couple and their friends to parties and picnics.[181] For their visit to French Oceania, Molly obtained a license in Papeete on the island of Tahiti, permitting her to drive an automobile, "Modèle A."[182] They had cabled ahead to Papeete to hire a house and a cook,[179] and registered there as residents on August 20, John being listed as "artiste peintre."[182] About a month later, on September 13, they

65. BANANA BLOSSOMS, *ca.* 1928, cat. no. 5.

66. LUSH FOLIAGE, *ca.* 1928, cat. no. 65.

moved to Pare Pirae, Tahiti, and on October 26 they arrived back in San Francisco aboard His Royal Majesty's Ship *Maunganui*.[182]

John brought back a collection of still lifes for which he would become particularly well known. These were portrayals of bananas in various stages of maturity, as well as enchanting tropical depictions of land and seascapes.

Molly had become a British subject upon her marriage to John in 1922. Six years later on November 7, 1928, while she and Shawn were in San Francisco "on business"[183] she was granted a Certificate of Naturalization to become a citizen once more of the United States. John O'Shea became a citizen in 1930.[184]

The Carmel Art Association, originally derived from the Art Chapter of the Carmel Club of Arts and Crafts, had its initial meeting on August 8, 1927.[185] It was held, like previous gatherings of artists, at the studio of painter Josephine M. Culbertson (1852–1939), like O'Shea, also a former student of the Adelphi Academy in Brooklyn, New York.[186] Although not recorded, John O'Shea was probably among the artists present. He was to be a very active member for the rest of his life. O'Shea is first mentioned in the Association's minutes of the meeting of January 24, 1928. He was elected a juror of paintings to be submitted at the next exhibition of the Association. Again in June 1929 he was chosen juror for the July–August exhibition, indicating the Association's early respect for his judgment.[187] Also shown and well received, were two of his own works, *Tahitian Bananas* and *Superstition Mountains*.

"John O'Shea as a painter of integrity and dynamic power is too well known to need any description."
Announcement of the opening of the Denny-Watrous Gallery, *Carmel Pine Cone*, March 20, 1931.

67 and 68. John and Molly O'Shea, *ca.* 1930. Photographs by Edward Weston, Carmel.

Posing, Painting, and Partying

69

"*The portrait of John O'Shea by Theodore Criley is a perfectly normal piece of work. Quietly painted and with no effort at jazz effects, it should prove a rock to cling to for many people who are absolutely dazed by the color and compositions of the modernists.*"

The Carmelite, April 25, 1928.

69. Theodore M. Criley, Double Portrait: JOHN O'SHEA AND MYSELF, *ca.* 1926, oil on canvas, 30″ × 25″, Coll. Richard Criley, Carmel.

Nineteen twenty-nine was a special year for John O'Shea. Accepting his stated birth year as 1879, he would celebrate his fiftieth birthday in 1929.

Judging from existing studio portraits by well-known professional photographers, John O'Shea was not adverse to posing. Previously mentioned were Genthe's portraits of Shawn and Molly while in New York City for their marriage in 1922. A somewhat later picture was taken by Ording.[188] In 1930 Edward Weston, then living in Carmel, studied and photographed both Shawn and Molly and commented on their sittings in his daybook.[189]

Weston had done Molly O'Shea the year before, not long after he arrived in Carmel. In connection with Mrs. O'Shea's sitting on May 1, 1929, he commented: "I have a feeling I am to do well here."[190] Later, in February 1930, he did both Shawn and Molly at their Highlands home, commenting, "real persons both of them! Evidently well-to-do which hasn't hurt them, indeed they are amongst few, one might say, whom money has enriched—added to their inherent charm."[191] Somewhat later[192] that year and the next, Edward Weston would record considerable dissatisfaction with John's temper, behavior, and even status as a painter. Nevertheless, O'Shea, as we shall see, did *buy* Weston's work, if not his praise! Sybil Brainard Anikeeff (also known as Anikeff or Anikeyev),[193] the portrait photographer and wife of Russian singer Vasia Anikeyef, produced a portrait of a handsome and virile O'Shea about 1935.

O'Shea sat as well for a portrait in oil by Theodore Criley. This painting and one of Peggy Williams, the wife of newspaperman and playwright Michael W. Williams, were exhibited in 1928 at the Fiftieth Annual Exhibition of the San Francisco Art Institute. A curious and interesting companion piece to the portrait of O'Shea, not exhibited, is a self-portrait of Criley in which he is painting his own portrait; the portrait of his friend O'Shea hangs behind him, both likenesses depicted in a mirror image (plate 69).

A clay or plaster bust, possibly a self-portrait, was made of O'Shea about 1950; its whereabouts is unknown, but two photographs of it, which were in O'Shea's possession, exist (see plate 170).

Quite accidentally, the only known sculpture by John O'Shea was discovered while searching for the identity of the artist for the clay bust and the whereabouts of the bust itself. It was thought[28] that D. Kirke Erskine of Carmel Highlands, a friend of O'Shea, was the sculptor. While Erskine was not the artist, he did mention owning a statue by O'Shea, generally thought to be the likeness of George Bernard Shaw,[194] which stood for many years outdoors on a pedestal at the O'Sheas' "Cliff Property." Further research revealed, in fact, that O'Shea had entered this cut-direct sandstone bust and an oil painting in The Exhibition of Painting and Sculpture at the Monterey County Fair, September–October 1931. Possibly "G.B.S." himself would have enjoyed the critic's comments on both of these works on that occasion:

70. JUNGLE STREAM, *ca.* 1928, cat. no. 60.

71. GEORGE BERNARD SHAW or ANCIENT PROPHET, Coll. D. Kirke Erskine, Carmel, cat. no. 306. Photograph, 1984.

71

70

John O'Shea's stone sculpture, which looks like a portrait of an ancient prophet, is attracting attention . . . Then there is John O'Shea's warm, tropical painting, vivid and interesting, of "Hawaiian Lei-Maker." Not the svelte, slim seductive Hawaiian we read about, but one whose avoir-dupois is appreciably painted under the modern dress and hot, scattered sunshine[195] (plates 71, 72).

"Than him there are few more modest artists." So wrote Ella Winter about John O'Shea in April 1929 in *The Carmelite*.[196] She and her husband, Lincoln Steffens, were among the founders of this popular Peninsula literary publication and were good friends of Shawn and Molly O'Shea. Ella Winter was publicizing an interview which she had had with the writer Frederick J. O'Brien after his visit with John O'Shea and his viewing of O'Shea's recent scenes of the South Seas. No one, apparently, had yet seen the Tahitian paintings and especially the banana series. Recently arrived in Carmel, O'Brien had lived for many years in Sausalito, California, but visited Carmel often.[197] He related to these paintings as few others could, having made extensive visits to those faraway places about which he wrote so eloquently in *White Shadows in the South Seas*. The book was then in the process of being made into a movie.

O'Brien's praise of O'Shea's work, together with Winter's compliment on his personality, are quite in contrast to Edward Weston's private impressions

72. LEI WOMAN, Coll. Anne Dickman-Grant, cat. no. 62. Photograph courtesy Anne Dickman-Grant.

73. TAHITIAN (youth), *ca.* 1928, cat. no. 107.

72

"Sean showed a number of paintings I had not seen. He has a dazzling color sense, and often achieves fine form."

Nancy Newhall, *The Daybooks of Edward Weston, Volume II. California*, entry for February 25, 1930.

73

of John O'Shea, the man and his *œuvre*, in his daybook.[198] Understandably, Weston depended on clients like O'Shea who "has not only been very kind to me, but has helped materially to raise my economic status."[199] Thus, in a public critique of his work he was "obliged" [my quotes] to flatter O'Shea "trying to excuse a guilty conscience," while in the privacy of his daybook, Weston criticized O'Shea's ego and his ability as a painter. Praising in public, faulting in private appears to have been a pervasive habit of Weston's, which was frequently reflected in his daybook when referring to others, particularly to accomplished professionals, such as photographer Alfred Stieglitz, a onetime mentor.[200]

As to "raising (Weston's) economic status" O'Shea bought the first print sold of Weston's famous *Kelp* on March 16, 1930,[201] at which time he told Weston: "I am going to have a whole portfolio of your prints"—and indeed he did acquire many prints.[202] O'Shea's fascination with this aquatic plant was expressed later in his own work; a charcoal drawing, *Kelp Garden*, was shown at the California Palace of the Legion of Honor in 1934 but remains unlocated today.

Weston, perhaps, should never have accepted the task of reviewing O'Shea's paintings at the Denny-Watrous Gallery in Carmel in 1931,[203] for, after all, in 1930 he had written in his daybook the following: "I can't often respond to painting with my greater interest in photography—the most important medium of our day. Now I am speaking more honestly my mind."[204] Significantly, in private and public criticisms, what Weston did like about O'Shea's 1931 exhibition were his *Bananas*. It seems that Weston had seen artistic merit in this fruit since he "had done two negatives in 1927 and then was sidetracked"[205] until he found time to concentrate on them again in June

"'B. did his bananas like a cabbage,' he cried mentioning a well known painter. 'He didn't see them as separate fruits. You've separated them, and that is how one sees them through you,' he said, turning to O'Shea. 'I see my South Seas again.'"

Ella Winter with Frederick O'Brien visiting John O'Shea, *The Carmelite*, April 3, 1929.

1930, perhaps not accidentally after the publicity given O'Shea's 1928 depiction of bananas in Ella Winter's spring 1929 interview of Frederick O'Brien.

Of the many anecdotes recounted,[28] one, most revealing of John O'Shea's temperament can be placed with almost certainty at its time of occurrence. It involves playwright Sinclair Lewis (1885–1951) and the date was March 1930. Shawn and Molly were having a party at the "Cliff Property." Sinclair Lewis told John he had a check for a painting he wished to buy. He handed over the check with a remark: "That will buy you a lot of good Irish whiskey, John." O'Shea reacted by pushing Lewis into a tide pool, and as Lewis was climbing out, O'Shea tore up the check and said: "My painting won't be hanging in *your* house!"[28] The artist was perhaps on the defensive because of his well-known

74. TAHITIAN BANANAS NO. 2, ca. 1928, cat. no. 109.

75. HEART OF CYPRESS AT CLIFF, cat. no. 161.

76. BEARDED MAN, BANANA GROVE, ca. 1928, cat. no. 81.

75

76

and often excessive drinking, and he might have been annoyed too by the reference to his native country in this context; but most likely John was infuriated because of the equation of one of *his* paintings with an amount of whiskey—even good Irish whiskey.

The incident is interesting because it involves Lewis with a different set of friends than he had during his earlier stay in Carmel from 1909 to 1911. Then he was known to everybody as "Hal" or "Red," was still single,[206] and had not yet become famous and wealthy. In 1927 the *Carmel Pine Cone* stated: "Sinclair Lewis who earned but three dollars in six months at Carmel is now [a] National Institution."[207]

In spring 1930, Lewis was traveling with his wife, Dorothy Thompson,[208] and according to Ella Young[209] during her 1930 visit,[210] the party at O'Shea's, in addition to Ella, consisted of Dorothy Thompson and Sinclair Lewis, Mabel and Tony Luhan, Robinson and Una Jeffers, and Lincoln Steffens and his wife, Ella Winter. Curiously, although Ella Young describes the brilliant repartee at this party, she fails to mention O'Shea's temperamental treatment of Lewis—perhaps in deference to John, to whom she was most devoted. Perhaps, however, Ella Young and her hosts, the Luhans,[210] had left the party earlier and missed the encounter between Lewis and O'Shea. Lewis and his wife had been visiting in Monterey and were on their way to Los Angeles.[208] This was the year, incidentally, that Lewis won and accepted the Nobel Prize for Literature—he had refused the Pulitzer in 1926.

Shawn and Molly enjoyed and collected oriental art. Much of their collection is intact today and proudly displayed by Molly's great-niece, Molly Jeppson. No doubt some of these items were acquired during the O'Sheas' sojourns in the South Seas and Hawaii, but they apparently collected artifacts on the mainland as well. In January 1930 they were offered prints, one by Hiroshige, by a G. A. Scott of Hollywood.[211] In Scott's letter we learn that John was planning a trip to Arizona—perhaps another time since 1927—and was invited to stop in Hollywood en route. Theodore Criley did not share this excursion with O'Shea, having just returned from a lengthy trip "by motor" through Europe (1929–30).[64]

Shawn and Molly probably went on to New Mexico from Arizona on that excursion in 1930, for it was in spring of 1931 that paintings of places and people near Taos first appeared. Similar in style and size to *Pop Hart* and *Grandma*, painted eight years earlier, is the large portrait of *Old Mexican Woman* or *Blind Woman of Taos*, which may also have been titled *Old Midwife-Taos* (plate 77). It is a penetrating image of an elderly seated woman, dressed in what appears to be a nun's habit or nurse's garb, who gazes past the viewer in peaceful, perhaps slightly skeptical contemplation; her walking stick leans on the chair behind her. Like *Pop Hart* and *Grandma*, this work exhibits a strong kinship with portraits by Diego Velásquez and Edouard Manet, which by descent indicate more than casual affinity to the portraits on dark, almost void backgrounds executed by Robert Henri. Titles like *Landscape Near Taos*, *Town of Valdez*, or *Valdez*, located northeast of Taos[154] (plate 78), and *Marada*,[212] or *Penitente Marada* appear. The latter, no doubt, a worship place of the Penitentes, whose customs so intrigued Ella Young that she wrote about them after her visit to Taos, where she stayed with her friends Tony and Mabel Dodge Luhan.[213] While in New Mexico the O'Sheas also stayed at the home of the Luhans, a most hospitable couple, who divided their time between Taos and Carmel.[64]

77

77. BLIND WOMAN OF TAOS, *ca.* 1930, cat. no. 11.

78. VALDEZ, *ca.* 1930, cat. no. 123.

Much has been written about Mabel Dodge; she was both a writer and a renowned international social figure. Her second husband was the painter Maurice Sterne (1878–1957) with whom she left Paris in 1916 and her home and salon in New York City and moved to Taos. Sterne stayed only two years but Mabel remained on, and she and her third husband, Tony Luhan, continued to count among their visitors painters, writers, and intellectuals from all over the world. Her book, *Taos and Its Artists*, is a memorable tribute to many of those who frequented her Taos salon and were her friends. It was said that:

> ... her contributions to our community (Taos) are not mythical—for she enriched immeasurably the artistic and cultural life, not only of our Town but our Time.[214]

John Marin (1870–1953), for instance, was a guest of the Luhans in 1929 and again in 1930. The O'Sheas also visited in 1930. Mabel Luhan was outspokenly fond of them; both "the genius Shawn" and especially Molly, about whom she wrote an extraordinary tribute in *The Carmelite* in May 1930.[215]

O'Shea must have been drawn to Taos by the reputation of its "legendary artists," but also by the land—the brilliant colors, vast expanses, strong masses and shapes often juxtaposed—all ingredients of the decorative lyricism O'Shea often expressed in his work.

O'Shea painted his large *Blind Woman of Taos* here, but portraiture and people, which drew so many other artists to Taos, were not as important to him in Taos as they were to Robert Henri, for instance. Henri visited Taos from his base in Santa Fe in 1916, 1917 or 1918, and again in 1922, but "wherever he went, his subject was people."[216] Nor was the "story telling" image so often seen in paintings of the Taos group of interest to O'Shea. His positive qualities lay not in progressive art expression, as in the case of artist Joseph A. Fleck (1893–1977), who could be imbued one day with the scenes around him, reflect the environment in portraits, landscapes, and murals, and the next day move to Kansas City, abandoning the past "in favor of an experimental form more in keeping with the modern trend."[217] John O'Shea had gone to Taos in 1930 for new subject, not modern trend.

Theodore Morrow Criley died suddenly in Carmel in October 1930 at the age of fifty, leaving behind a loving family, a host of mourners, and a legacy of magnificent paintings. To this day his extensive artistic production remains for the most part carefully in storage and unrecorded. Its evaluation and recognition await public exposure, but will not be disappointing in its coming. Extraordinary beauty in form and color, together with skillful composition, are present on almost every canvas. For the present, the alliance of Theodore Criley's and John O'Shea's spirits is reflected in their paintings by their complementary, secure, and accomplished artistry.

79. PURPLE TREE, FALL NO. 2, cat. no. 192.

80. NEAR TAOS, *ca*. 1930, cat. no. 169.

81. FLOWERING HILLS, *ca*. 1933, cat. no. 44.

Tribute to this extraordinary man was paid by many who knew him. An article, which relates Criley's recent exposure to "Latins" during his long stay in Europe (especially Spain and France), includes a reference to John O'Shea:

> John O'Shea the great painter, his neighbor at the Highlands, was telling me of this not long ago: "His contact with the Latins has taught him something" he said, "To let life live itself a bit, instead of continuously hustling it along."[218]

A month after Criley's death, George William Russell (1867–1935) of Dublin, the Irish poet and economist known by his pen name Æ (a diphthong for Aeon according to Ella Young[219]), was the guest of the O'Sheas at "Tynalacan" for Thanksgiving in 1930.[220] Undoubtedly, Russell, a proficient landscape painter and a member of the Theosophical Society, was in California to visit the group's Headquarters in La Loma, near San Diego.

Although the date is uncertain, we do know that O'Shea painted in Hawaii. Two visits are surely indicated and possibly a third. One may have been during the O'Sheas' voyage on the *Makura* to the South Pacific, or when they returned to San Francisco aboard the R.M.S. *Maunganui* (October 26, 1928, see n. 182). Another time, according to an undated newspaper clipping, without source, "He and Mrs. O'Shea arrived Tuesday on the *Maui* to look over Hawaii and see what it has to offer in the way of scenery and particularly in the way of marine views." In addition we learn that "they brought with them their automobile."[221] A third visit is indicated by the existence of photographs showing the O'Sheas *together* with the Benjamin Pines on a ship voyage; the photographs were preserved along with postcards illustrating the *S.S. Mololo Entering Honolulu Harbor*. Also preserved is a postcard of *Night Blooming Cereus, Hawaii*.[222] A painting entitled *Night Blooming Cereus* was first exhibited in 1934 at the

"*hen he has made a sojourn in the South Seas and
eturned with vistas of the flamboyant vegetation
f the jungle-like regions of Honolulu and Oahu. To
ur colder northern senses these vistas would seem
ncredible, if they were not portrayed with such
anifest sincerity and vivacity.*"

:udio Gossip, *Carmel Pine Cone*, July 29, 1932.

82. RABBIT ISLAND OFF OAHU, HAWAII, *ca.* 1930, cat. no. 193.

83. GOLDEN HILLS, cat. no. 48.

82

California Palace of the Legion of Honor in San Francisco. Finally, there also exists a "vivid and beautiful" watercolor entitled *Cloud over Hawaii*, dated 1934; the dating itself is a rare occurrence.[223] The first mention of Hawaiian subjects appears in a newspaper clipping dated March 26, 1931.[224]

At the Denny-Watrous Gallery in Carmel, O'Shea was showing "paintings of Hawaiian beaches" *and* "many interesting landscapes of mountains and canyons" resulting from a "recent trip to Taos." The latter were no doubt the fruits of his trip to Arizona and New Mexico. This appears to be the first in a series of exhibitions which were mounted by his friends Dene Denny and Hazel Watrous in their galleries, now newly enlarged and with the addition of a small stage.[225] Edward Weston, writing on April 2, 1931, in *The Carmelite*, compares the "serene majesty" of one mountain, the *Pali* (Hawaii), with others, *Superstition Mountains* (Arizona), and a painting entitled the *Maine Coast*. Thereafter Hawaiian paintings appear frequently in exhibition reviews.

The O'Sheas spent the winter months 1931–32 in New York and Chicago, probably visiting familiar places and friends and perhaps Molly's family in Terre Haute, Indiana. On his return to California O'Shea said that he:

> found the Metropolitan Museum (New York City) and the Art Institute in Chicago desolate and neglected. Their empty, echoing corridors sounded a dreary knell in his heart. New York was in a deplorable condition. . . . The depression seemed to have hit everything but the theatres and public interest in artists and painters is waning. No one wants to look at exhibitions any more.[226]

O'Shea expressed pessimism and a downhearted feeling toward any exhibitions of his own work and "was not planning for any in the immediate future." But all of this dejection was probably a reaction to a hectic, tiring schedule in Carmel in 1931 and was soon to be forgotten as O'Shea commenced renewed and vigorous activities in the years ahead.

Also, a transcontinental voyage and a holiday stay of prolonged duration in New York and Chicago speaks well of the O'Sheas' financial security during those economically difficult times.

Very little activity is perceived during 1932. A "huge and sombre portrait" was shown at the annual exhibition of the Carmel Art Association in June. To a reviewer it "looks as though it belonged in some dull and dusty corridor of a museum"; and the writer wondered "why didn't he send over one of his Tahitian compositions?"[227] In August, nevertheless, John O'Shea, artist, is cited as being among those inducted into "Carmel's own Hall of Fame."[228]

When Shawn and Molly built "Tynalacan" in 1924, the hills around them were quite bare, most trees having been logged early in the century "when ships tied up at Notley's Landing down by Rocky Point [frontispiece], to take on logs for construction elsewhere."[28] As the years passed, nature and the landscaping around "palatial homes" which had sprouted in the Highlands led to a need to establish a fire protection district to combat the annual fires in the hills. John O'Shea was duly selected as an active fireman in 1932.[229]

To a reviewer in December, O'Shea's contribution to the Association's show at the Denny-Watrous Gallery was as puzzling as had been the portrait to the reviewer in June:

> O'Shea has two grotesque masses of ink which he failed to name; they are so unusual, perhaps no name could fit them. Yet they are interesting as experimental work of an artist."[230]

It seems clear that among the diverse reactions conveyed to readers by art critics reviewing John O'Shea's works during the twenty years since his first exhibition in Pasadena, boredom was not one.

84. TROPICAL FOLIAGE, *ca.* 1928, cat. no. 212.

85. CYPRESS AND SEA, cat. no. 145.

"The sea curls in waves behind him, sapphire-blue except where churning foam transfigures it to chalcedony."

Speaking of the view of the sea from the "Cliff Property": Ella Young, *Flowering Dusk*.

Shawn Shows at the Palace

Nineteen thirty-three brings us a new aspect of O'Shea's versatile art expression. In a preview Lincoln Steffens wrote in September 1932:

> He has been playing in black and white, and the fun of it sticks out like all creation, in every line, in every whole and in the way O'Shea shows the stuff that is in him.[231]

Beginning on February 14, 1933, about thirty charcoal paintings were exhibited at the Denny-Watrous Gallery to critical acclaim by the Peninsula press. Accustomed to facile brush strokes in glowing colors on large canvases, the viewers were exposed to an array of drawings of animals and people, "abstractions," as well as land and seascapes, mainly in black on white utilizing charcoal, crayon, and graphite with occasional coloration. Even Edward Weston, his frequent critic in private, urged his readers to: "go, do not miss this rare opportunity; receive your own reactions and leave, as you must be, enriched."[232]

86. WAVES ON ROCKS, cat. no. 243.

87

88

89

"Mr. O'Shea's medium in most of [these] compositions is a black chalk with which he seems able to get any effect he desires in line or tone. With this, a restrained use of color and large, uncluttered pattern areas, moving against one another, produce a design form that is capable of interpreting his monumental subject matter."

Patricia Cunningham in a newspaper clipping in the O'Shea scrapbook, no name, no date, but surely June 1945.

87. WHITE POOL, cat. no. 286.

88. FOAM, ROCKS AND COAST, cat. no. 258.

89. PORTRAIT; MAN IN WOODS, cat. no. 233.

90. NIGHT BLOOMING CEREUS, cat. no. 490, unlocated. Photograph by Edward Weston, Carmel.

To Mary Ada Reade of the *Monterey Peninsula Herald*, some of the abstractions and drawings were disconcerting—attributed to John O'Shea's need for amusement during the rainy season and perhaps even being the effects of the continual steam shoveling in connection with the construction of the new highway[233] which was eventually to run between his house and studio. Una Jeffers was quite pleased with the numerous works. About the charcoal drawings and their abstract nature she remarked:

> These 'experiments' of his, however, have the power to bring those seeing them that instantaneous quickening and enhancement of life that is the chief function of true art.[234]

It was at this exhibition that the grotesque "imaginative painting, done in color," of his friend Lincoln Steffens was unveiled to the public. The *Oakland Tribune* wrote jokingly that this figure, entitled *His Soul*, which had caused a sensation in Steffens's hometown, "may spread to other art circles of the country."[235] It is difficult to comprehend today the impact of the writings of a "muckraker" like Steffens and how daring it must have been to criticize him, even in jest and especially as a close personal friend!

In March at the Oakland (California) Art Gallery, O'Shea showed *Young Bananas* in the Exhibition of Works of Western Artists.

Not one to hesitate to show earlier work, O'Shea in September exhibited a "brilliant group of pictures" at the prestigious Hotel Del Monte Art Gallery in Monterey and again in November at the Thomas Welton Stanford Gallery at Stanford University, Palo Alto.[15,236] A reviewer in the *Carmel Pine Cone* com-

91.

mented that among the approximately twenty-six paintings were "striking original and stimulating"²³⁷ works from the desert, Tahiti, and Hawaii.

Not mentioned in this review dealing with a number of flower paintings is the work entitled *Night Blooming Cereus* discussed earlier in connection with possible visits to Hawaii. While its location today is unknown, we are fortunate to have two photographic prints which indicate that it is in oil on canvas (plate 90). One marked in O'Shea's handwriting indicates its title and the fact that the photograph is by Edward Weston. The other bears the stamp of John Douglas Short.

It is likely that these photographs, like others, were prepared for publicity purposes in connection with the forthcoming exhibition of O'Shea's paintings at the California Palace of the Legion of Honor in San Francisco.²⁵³ Dated November 2, 1934, the following critique of *Night Blooming Cereus* by Short, a lawyer, writer, and friend of O'Shea, heightens one's curiosity about the work and one's regret that the painting has been lost:

> Some one has said that O'Shea, even though he had never painted, would be potentially one of the great artists. You readily sense, from his pictures, the reason for this remark, for the best of them are alive with feeling and reveal an emotional content that is almost fervent at times, as in his huge studies of tropical bananas; and at others intangible, faint and evanescent, as in the exquisite painting of the Night Blooming Cereus. . . . His work has surprising variety and freshness and he uses color with generous delight, but with an informed and perfect choice.
>
> The small show at the Denny-Watrous Gallery in Carmel is a fine collection and creditably represents some of this most versatile artist's work; he is unquestionably one of the few important men painting in the West today.²³⁸

O'Shea's firsthand familiarity with flowers, obtained through his interest in gardening, is documented. On a number of occasions he was asked to design garden beds and arrange plantings in front of the Carmel Art Association building on Dolores Street²³⁹ and in his last years he wrote fondly of trees, ferns, magnolias, camellias and many other plants in letters to his sister-in-law Emma Pine.²⁴⁰ It is not surprising, therefore, that he would also paint flowers, and many of these works are well documented. They vary from the hibiscus behind the ear of the handsome *Tahitian Youth*, surely 1928 (plate 91), to *Mixed Flowers* ("a vase of multicolored flowers against a brilliant green-yellow background"), a large oil painting shown on a number of occasions, including the memorial exhibition in Carmel the year he died.²⁴¹ He painted the previously mentioned *Night Blooming Cereus* and *Calla Lilies* (or *Yellow Callas*?) about 1934; *Dahlias*, *Birds of Paradise* (plate 92), *Cosmos*, as well as approximately seven versions of bananas, all depicting the blossom in various developmental stages (plates 65, 74, 95). In addition to these still lifes, O'Shea painted landscapes entitled variously, *Poppies and Lupins*, *Apple Blossoms*, *Pear Blossoms*,²⁴² *The Flamboyant* (Tahiti or Hawaii—"a whirl of scarlet bloom against the vivid blue of tropic skies"),²⁴³ and additional orchard scenes (plates 93, 94).

A notable range of techniques is seen in these flower portraits, varying from the Impressionist, perhaps Manet-inspired, loosely painted *Night Blooming Cereus* to the tightly painted, almost stylized *Birds of Paradise*, which bears strong geometric design, a stylized swan in the form of a vase, egrets decorating the screen, and glazed table top—all characteristic emblems of Art Deco.²⁴⁴

Affairs of the Carmel Art Association occupied much of O'Shea's time early in 1934. He was the President of the Association when papers of incorporation were executed on January 20. When they were filed on February 5, John O'Shea of Carmel Highlands signed as Director and remained in that position while Armin Carl Hansen became the first President of the incorporated Association on February 9.⁸⁶

91. TAHITIAN YOUTH, PORTRAIT, *ca.* 1928, cat. no. 112.

92. BIRD OF PARADISE, *ca.* 1931, cat. no. 10.

92

In February 1934 John O'Shea contributed a painting to an auction at the Women's City Club of San Francisco for the benefit of the National Committee for the Defense of Political Prisoners, chaired by Lincoln Steffens. The items contributed by a long list of prominent citizens were auctioned by actor James Cagney.[245] In March O'Shea, Ritschel, Hansen, Dougherty, and other members donated paintings for a raffle to benefit the Carmel Art Association. Armin Hansen conducted the raffle.[246]

Undoubtedly, however, the artist's attention during these and the following weeks was concentrated on preparation for his one-man exhibition at the California Palace of the Legion of Honor in San Francisco. Originally scheduled for February to March, it was postponed until April and May.[247] It appears that this exhibition came about either through invitation by the museum, a friend, or an associate thereof rather than on the artist's own initiative. Although purely conjectural, Albert Maurice Bender, the San Francisco businessman, financier, philanthropist, and art patron, may have played a role in this matter. A native of Dublin, Ireland, and the son of a Jewish rabbi,[248] Bender came to San Francisco in 1879 when he was thirteen.[249] Over the years, Bender was to become one of San Francisco's foremost art patrons. He donated a staggering

93. FLOWERING ORCHARD, cat. no. 45.

94. FRUIT TREES, cat. no. 46.

"*There is a sound of bees in the valley as we descend. There is a fragrance of orchard trees and stream-delighting willows . . .*"

Ella Young, *Flowering Dusk*.

93

94

number of art works to many institutions, showing "his perspicacity and instinct for uncovering, fostering and appreciating genius"[250] in many fields of art. He was, for instance, the person who first sponsored prints by Ansel Adams.[251] One might logically imagine that Bender was O'Shea's liaison to the Legion of Honor, especially since prior to the exhibition Bender had already purchased three of O'Shea's works for later presentation to the Municipal Art Gallery in Dublin.[252]

Fortunately, almost the entire correspondence relating to this exhibition has been located.[253] In it we discovered that the instigator was not Bender, but

95. BANANA FOLIAGE, *ca.* 1928, cat. no. 6.

the San Francisco philanthropist, singer, friend of writers and musicians, nephew of Senator Phelan and, somewhat later, resident of "Hollow Hills Farm" in Carmel Valley—Noël Sullivan. Sullivan shared with Albert Bender the title of "The Prince of San Francisco."[254] Noël Sullivan saw O'Shea's work in May 1933, wrote about it to Lloyd Leroy Rollins, the Director of the Legion of Honor,[255] who had also just seen the collection. Rollins wrote back to Sullivan that he was "sure that the gorgeous color and design of Mr. O'Shea's canvases will make a tremendous impression with the San Francisco public."[256] Thereafter, we have an exchange of letters between Thomas Carr Howe, Jr., then Assistant Director of the California Palace of the Legion of Honor, and Ella

"His forms pile up ecstatically, his colors heighten themselves, canyons cut into mountains with great sculptural movement."
Arthur Millier, *The Argus*, March 1928.

96. GRAND CANYON NO. 1, *ca.* 1930, cat. no. 49.

Young.[257] Molly hurriedly composed a biographical sketch of Shawn, which except for a few notations on envelopes or labels, is the only known example of serious writing by Molly O'Shea in existence.[15] Whatever the case, it must have been considered an honor then, as it is today, to be asked to exhibit one's work in such auspicious surroundings.

Wherever John O'Shea was taught the basic rules of technically preparing a painting, he learned his lesson well. His oils are to this day rarely flawed by flaking, indicating quality materials and proper sizing; the support is superb linen canvas or good cotton fabric, the stretchers are of good quality—if not always squared—and intended to be professionally framed. The substrates for his works on paper are in general of good quality.

It is known that O'Shea invariably gave much thought to the way in which his work was exhibited, giving not only personal attention to the choice of frames—of which he was known to have ordered many custom-made and expensive ones[28]—but to related matters such as transportation and insurance as well. For the "black and whites" to be shown, special celluloid material covering was ordered through the Legion of Honor.[15] The San Francisco show, ultimately listing sixty-three pieces, must have been a major concern of O'Shea's, if only in terms of logistics.

Two galleries were occupied by his art; "one filled with oils and the other with black and whites and a small overflow of oils and watercolors."[258] Not since 1928, his previous one-man exhibition in San Francisco, was there so much written about O'Shea in the Bay Area and Monterey Peninsula press. Shawn and Molly were in San Francisco to hang the exhibition and stayed at the Western Women's Club Hotel, where they welcomed interviewers. Some took advantage and "got a thumb nail view of the artist and his work."[259]

The reporter from the *San Francisco Chronicle* recorded these comments about O'Shea:

> Quiet, humorous, finding it difficult to talk about himself, he sat in the window of his suite . . . The 'soaking in' process, he admitted, with a smile for his wife, takes him so long sometimes as to quite exhaust her patience. "And then I paint—frantically—what I see. And I capture something while the vision is fresh and not hampered by a frozen technique," he said.
> "Yes, he paints at white hot heat and the air's blue with curses" interjected Mrs. O'Shea. A certain rhythm and freedom in style, the artist said, is due to his method of handling his brush, after the fashion of the Chinese, between thumb and first finger.
> His use of black and white is his 'inevitable reaction from color.'
> He likes best of all to do character studies and portraits from memory.
> When he isn't painting he has several hobbies—all of them highly dangerous to the precious hands of the artist. They are building walls, cutting stone, trimming trees and gardening.
> It keeps the nerves steady, the muscles strong, and then like an Italian workman, one can drink his wine, eat his spaghetti and sleep.[259]

To another reporter, however, O'Shea "is the most retiring and reticent of artists."[260]

Essentially a retrospective of O'Shea's work, the exhibition at the Legion of Honor included not only oils and watercolors, his customary media, but a number in a variety of different techniques and styles that he had created since the Beaux Arts Galerie show of 1928. These included charcoal drawings, "abstractions," spontaneous animal drawings and portraits, and a series of watercolors executed on the hard, flat, and very smooth surface of a Masonite-like material, perhaps an early type of Formica. H. L. Dungan of the *Oakland Tribune* commented on this type of work—two, perhaps three, examples of which are known today, *The Peak* and *Ghost Forest* (plates 100, 101), the latter dated 1934, and *Cypress and Ocean*—as follows:

> They are painted on a smooth, hard composition, giving the watercolor the strength of oil combined with its own delicacy. This manner of handling watercolor is a new experiment with O'Shea and a most successful one.[258]

Junius Cravens of the *San Francisco News* summed up this versatility:

> But for the true artist, subject is only a means to an end. One feels that O'Shea is first and always an artist. And he is a painter "what is" [sic] a painter. That he is ever experimenting, ever feeling his way along new paths, is evident not only in his oils but also and more particularly in his drawings in charcoal. Consequently his approach, whether it be to landscape or still life, portrait or abstraction is fresh and vigorous.[261]

In contrast, the critic from *The Argonaut* wrote: "The harder I tried, the more I didn't like them."[262]

86

97

98

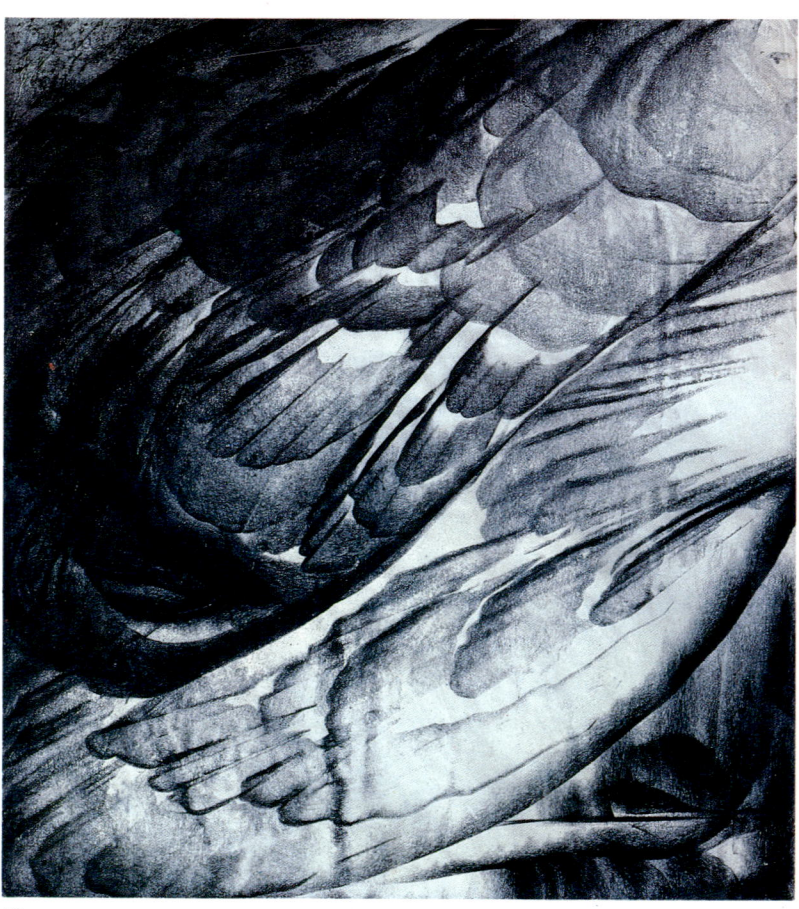
99

97. VORTEX, cat. no. 242.

98. ABSTRACTION: GEOMETRICS (NO. 3), *ca.* 1933, cat. no. 218.

99. ABSTRACTION: GRAVEN SANDSTONE (NO. 1), *ca.* 1933, cat. no. 219.

100

"O'Shea has painted as originally and as independently as if there were no other artists in the world working toward the same goal."

Robert H. Wilson for the *San Francisco Bulletin*, quoted in *The Carmelite*, April 11, 1928.

101

100. THE PEAK, *ca.* 1934, cat. no. 175.

101. GHOST FOREST, 1934, cat. no. 154.

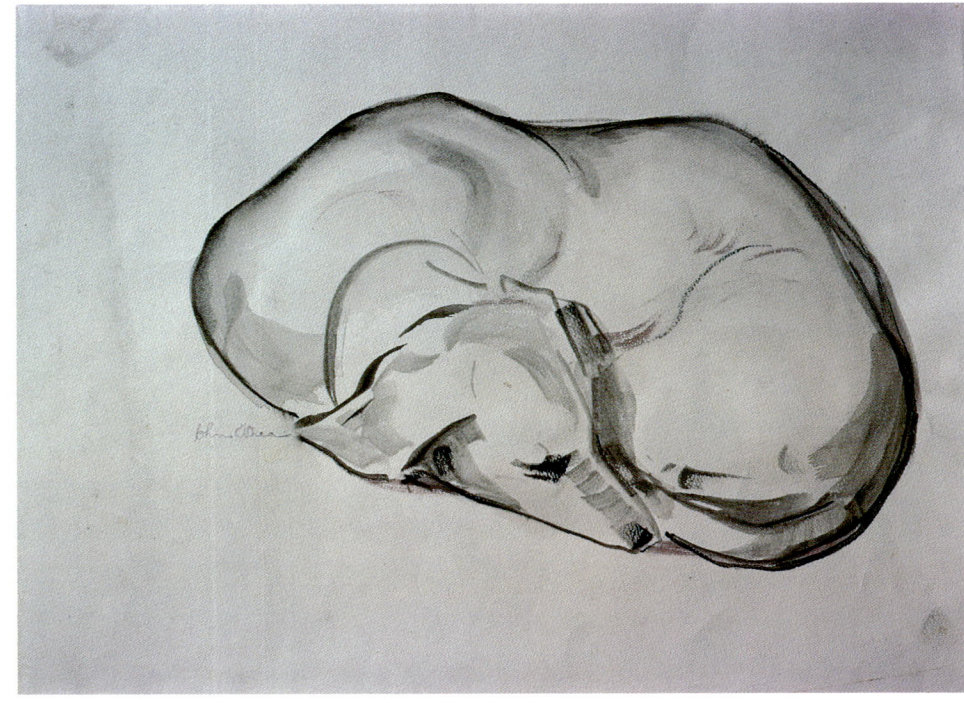

103

102

102. STORKS, cat. no. 208.

103. LEDA IN REPOSE (Police dog), cat. no. 167.

This seems an appropriate place to interject a few comments about John O'Shea's affection for animals. On the list of items exhibited,[263] those purchased by Bender and the *Portrait of the late George ("Pop") Hart* are not priced. The only item marked "Not for Sale" is *Leda in Repose* (number 42). On February 22, 1930, after he had gone to photograph Molly and Shawn at their Highlands home, Edward Weston wrote that "while working I noted Leda, their police dog, asleep in a most beautiful posture, and made three negatives, which I look forward to with great interest."[264] Whether Weston ever printed these is not known, but we believe that O'Shea's drawing of *Leda in Repose* still exists (plate 103). Other animal paintings in the exhibition were *Goat* (lent by Mrs. Douglas Short), *Wild Horse* (lent by Edward Weston), *Cock*, and possibly *Madame Bunny*. *Cock*, then owned by Mrs. Theodore Criley, is extant. Of it Ella Young wrote: "There was a fighting cock in the attitude of challenging—a delicate and subtle—life and fight in every feather of him."[265]

Goats were also sketched by O'Shea a number of times. Ella Young, Molly, and Shawn once visited Noël Sullivan (who eventually raised a whole herd of goats and sheep[266]) on his "twenty acres huddled in a hollow of the hills" above Carmel Valley, and while there they visited Noël's "long-eared Nubian goats." Ella wrote:

> Loitering in the afternoon sunshine among the flowers, we admire the fountain and its lilies. John speaks of goats, and we troop to the mountain-pasture where they have assembled themselves. There are goats a-plenty, and with them sheep enough to remind one of the scriptural parable. John moves affably among them, but disdains a sketch-book. He feels sure that he can envisage those countenances and those sleek bodies. He is learned in their ways, he is experienced in the moods and manners of goats. He can show them at will: grave or sprightly, friendly or cynical—long-eared, short-tailed, black, white, and yellow[267]

That goats (and fowl!) still fascinate artists today was apparent in a 1984 exhibition, *Morris Graves: Vision of the Inner Eye*, at The Oakland Museum. Graves's *Hero—Portrait of the Irish Celtic Temperament*, 1955, is reminiscent of O'Shea's sketches of goats. Depicted in the accompanying catalogue (plate 114), this work is said to show the symbolic use "of a proud old goat" in connection with Irish Authority.

104

105

"In this idea he is heartened by Molly and by myself, chiefly, I think, because we admire John's work so much and are really curious to see what goats would look like on John's canvas."

Ella Young, *Flowering Dusk*.

104. EQUINE FRIEND, cat. no. 150.

105. SOW, cat. no. 256.

106. HUNGRY GOAT, cat. no. 164.

106

90

107

Even after Molly's death, their last pet, a dachshund named "Kirschel," lived with O'Shea in Carmel Woods and was frequently photographed with him.[268] When Kirschel died she was buried there near a big magnolia tree[269] (plate 107).

Neither the details of their meeting nor when Bender first saw works by John O'Shea are known, but apparently Bender purchased several on more than one occasion. As mentioned previously, a copy of the list of works shown at the California Palace of the Legion of Honor indicates that three charcoal drawings, *Old Cypress Trunk* (No. 37), *Abstraction* (No. 38), and *Nocturne* (No. 47), were "For the National Museum of Ireland, Gift of Albert M. Bender." On May 6, 1934, the *Oakland Tribune* reported that one drawing, "an old cypress tree, or rather, merely part of the trunk, gnarled and twisted," has been purchased by Bender for the "Irish National Museum, Dublin." A note on this subject in *Controversy*, dated November 2, 1934, stated that Bender "has within the past few weeks, acquired three fine examples of John O'Shea's work in black and whites. One is a huge study of a negro head, another is the toiling grotesqueness of an ancient oak and the third the sort of weird thrilling life O'Shea leads under the sea."[250] An Irish paper—probably the *Irish Independent*, Dublin, no date—said that "Mr. Albert Bender, of San Francisco . . . has just presented some pictures (by 'one of the foremost artists on the Pacific Coast') to the Municipal Art Gallery."[270]

108

107. Molly and John with Kirschel, *ca.* May 1941.

108. REDWOOD BASES, cat. no. 196.

109. CITYSCAPE, cat. no. 227.

These various reports notwithstanding, the Hugh Lane Municipal Gallery of Modern Art in Dublin has today in its permanent collection three works by John O'Shea: *Fish*, a watercolor; *Colourman* and *Tree Bark*, both charcoal on paper. Curiously, while only the *Fish* painting was accepted at the Gallery's Art Advisory Committee meeting on January 17, 1935, all three works were retained and registered as gifts from Mr. Bender.[271] It is significant and in keeping not only with Bender's magnanimity, but with his wide circle of friends as well, that Eamon De Valera, then president of the executive council of the government of Ireland under the Fianna Fail party,[272] had just months before "delivered a dedicatory address upon the occasion of the acceptance of a collection as the 'Augusta Bender Memorial Collection of Oriental Art'" at the National Museum in Dublin.[250,271] Augusta was Mr. Bender's mother.

Finally, as further evidence of Bender's interest in the work of O'Shea, we read that Albert M. Bender has in his personal collection O'Shea's Mexican study *Head Man of the Village*, and an entry in the files of Ferdinand Perret[273] states that O'Shea was represented in the Albert M. Bender Collection of San Francisco (founded in 1937)[274] by two works: *Man in Stove Pipe Hat*, a charcoal, and *Portrait of a Mexican*, an oil. Their locations are unknown today. Assuming that these three items had been among the 1,100 works of art that Bender donated to the San Francisco Museum of Art, they may have been among the "many of which, unfortunately, [were] deaccessioned in the early 1970s in two major local sales."[275]

Leaving San Francisco after what must have been a gratifying tribute to twenty years of painting in California, the West, and the Pacific, Shawn and Molly left on a motor tour to the north along the Redwood Highway.[259] Perhaps the famous Sonoma and Napa Valley wine country was part of their itinerary. A penciled title for *Sonoma Winery Barns*, initialed "J.O'S." on a piece of cardboard, is known, and although the painting is not, it appears to have been a large watercolor or drawing.

In August 1934 preparations were underway on the Monterey Peninsula for the big Bal Masqué at the Del Monte Hotel. John O'Shea was among the "Names of International Importance" listed for this large gathering of artists in September.[276]

In October 1934 the Denny-Watrous Gallery in Carmel again honored O'Shea. As before when it had reopened on Dolores Street in 1931, the walls of the new gallery on San Carlos Street were resplendent with paintings—now twenty in number, in various media[238]—no doubt reflecting his recent success at San Francisco. "No showing could be better chosen for the first offering on the walls of the freshly decorated gallery."[277] Simultaneously, O'Shea exhibited "an interesting group at the [Carmel Art Association] Gallery as well"—the medium being "black and white."[278] Finally, at the end of a busy year O'Shea displayed four "smaller canvases" at the Art Association Gallery: "an interesting child's head and three tropical studies; a Tahitian village, a flower painting and one of gaudy tropical fish."[279]

The strength of his continued interest in watercolor as a means of expressing his motivation in art was presented in a critique of his entries for the January 1935 Watercolor Exhibit at the Art Gallery in Carmel:

> A leader in the experimental and highly individualistic field of the local art group is John O'Shea. He is off on some path of his own; he is discovering something within himself and new art truths. If you cannot understand him or agree with him, you can respect him for he is doing something definite and purposeful, not just messing about. It does not quite come off every time, of course. His two paintings in the January show are an example of one that does and one that doesn't.[280]

"'Tahitian Fish'... a beautiful piece of work simply and masterfully done."

Monte, "Art Exhibit Best in History of Association, says Critic," *Carmel Pine Cone*, January 11, 1929.

In February 1935 at the Carmel Art Association Gallery, "the trend toward modern is noted . . . [John O'Shea] shows how that unpredictable desert country around Taos affected him. High, brash desert light and luminous blue sky . . ."[281] Then in March while "John O'Shea shows another of his lush, tropical landscapes and a gorgeous study of yellow callas in a polished brass bowl of beautiful shape" at Carmel,[282] the Kingsley Art Club of Sacramento, California, which began sponsoring annual exhibitions of contemporary art in 1927,[275] presented twenty-one of O'Shea's canvases at the E. B. Crocker Art Gallery (now Crocker Art Museum). An interesting commentary on O'Shea's technique appeared in one of the Sacramento papers the day after the opening of the exhibition:

> More delicate in coloring is the Hawaiian seascape *Inside the Reef*. The jade and sapphire green of the sea is divided from the prismatic colors of the sky by a thin white wave breaking over the reef. Touches of the bare canvas show through. This is true of some of the other paintings in which the artist seems to be using watercolor technique, the paint being very thin.[283]

While we are not intent on classifying this and contemporaneous works of O'Shea as purely Impressionist, it is nevertheless a coincidence that certain aspects of this Impressionist technique should be discussed in a similar manner in the following excerpt from the *Crocker Art Museum Handbook of Paintings* (1979). The work under discussion is *Sketching*, a well-known painting by O'Shea's contemporary, Mary Amanda Lewis (1877–1953), probably painted under the tutelage of William Merritt Chase (1849–1916) during his painting classes in Carmel in 1914:

> This work certainly reflects Chase's dictum to paint spontaneously from nature. The example of French Impressionism seems also to be reflected here in the manner with which broken strokes of color are used to suggest sun-dappled foliage and figures. The impromptu nature of the outdoor scene and the sketchy application of paint which allows the white canvas to show through reinforce the supposition that the artist was familiar with the procedures of Impressionist painting.[284]

110. CALM BAY, cat. no. 262.

111. TROPICAL FISH, Coll. Molly Jeppson, cat. no. 121.

112. INSIDE THE REEF, *ca.* 1931, cat. no. 59.

2

". . . the magic of a Hawaiian landscape, 'Within the Reef,' rich in natural color—jade inside the reef, sapphire without."

Ada Hanifin, *San Francisco Examiner*, May 6, 1934.

113. BIRCHES, cat. no. 9.

Unfortunately, only two of O'Shea's early "impressionistic" works in oil are known today—*Seascape; Sea Clouds* (plate 8) and *Eucalyptus Trees in Storm* (or *Revelry*) (plate 1)—although a good deal was written about these paintings during his Pasadena-Laguna Beach period.[32] But he must, in fact, have been familiar with these "procedures."

"O'Shea belongs to that rather rare class of folk for whom, in the words of Theophile Gautier, 'The visible world really exists.' His canvases are a revelation . . ."

Carmel Pine Cone, July 29, 1932.

Hecho en Mexico

114

114. HILLS, FURROWS AND TRUNK, cat. no. 163.

While the Sacramento exhibition was still in progress, the O'Sheas closed their Carmel Highlands home[285] and departed for Mexico, probably accompanied, as mentioned earlier, by their friends and neighbors the "D. L." Jameses. Planning to stay three months,[285] they stayed for six.[286]

During his absence John O'Shea's *Desert Village* was shown at the June exhibition at the Carmel Art Gallery under the headline "Sun over Taos." The painting is addressed as "New Mexico under full sun with a peculiarly luminous desert sky."[287]

It is recalled that Molly spent some time in Mexico as a young woman,[64] and that because of her beauty, she "occasionally attracted a lot of attention at the 'corridas.'" Also, it is supposed that "Tynalacan," the name Molly gave their home, was of Mexican origin and probably had some special significance. The itinerary of their Mexican visit is not known, but one speculates that Molly, having no doubt lived in Aguascalientes, the attractive colonial city where her first husband had been United States Consul in 1907, might have suggested a visit there en route to Mexico City. Perhaps the famous Spring Festival attracted their attention. The festival is celebrated today from late April to early May and includes an art exposition.

A handwritten list of paintings and drawings exists which coincides almost exactly with the twenty-eight works of "Subjects of Mexico" exhibited one year later at the Del Monte Art Gallery in Monterey.[288] The list is written on the stationery of the Hotel Imperial at Guadalajara. According to the stationery, the hotel featured: "Sixty Rooms, Sixty Baths and Sixty Telephons [sic]; No Better Climate Anywhere, and American and European Plan!"[289]

A photograph of the O'Sheas and Jameses with "D. L." emerging from a stone structure was taken at pre-Conquest ruins in Mexico (plate 117). The structure is apparently the Coatepantl or wall of snakes' heads around the Teocali in Mexico City.[290] Also, the photograph seems to have been developed at "Madero 34 • Mexico," according to a faintly legible stamp on the reverse of the print. (Avenida Madero is a main street in downtown Mexico City.)

The title of "subject number 7," *Woman of Taxco*, in the Del Monte Art Gallery's 1936 exhibition of "Subjects of Mexico," indicates the O'Sheas—and perhaps the Jameses—went on to Taxco so that John could paint. From the handwritten prices in the extant checklist one assumes that *Woman of Taxco* was a large painting, the price being $500. The whereabouts of a painting by this name is unknown today. Perhaps a study of it was the "arresting study of a Mexican woman lent by its owner, Mrs. D. L. James of the Highlands" in 1945 to a June exhibition of drawings by John O'Shea at the Carmel Art Association.[291] (Mrs. James is now deceased.) Or it may be the exquisite portrait of which "the donor is Miss Edith Dickinson of Sausalito, who has given (in 1962 to the Memorial Art Gallery in City Hall) the painting depicting a Mexican girl in memory of her father, the late Henry F. Dickinson of Carmel Point."[292] This

96

115

116

117

118

115. MEXICAN SALESWOMAN, *ca.* 1935, Coll. Molly Jeppson, cat. no. 259.

116. GRAY SHAWL, cat. no. 157.

117. The O'Sheas (left and right) and the D. L. Jameses in Mexico, *ca.* 1935.

118. WOMEN IN SHAWLS, cat. no. 297.

119

119. COMIDA, MARKET DAY, *ca.* 1936, Coll. Harrison Memorial Library, cat. no. 27.

painting, entitled *Mexican Girl*, now hangs in the City Hall Council Chamber in Carmel (see plate 122).

Both *Mexican Girl* (29½" × 25") and a larger one, *Comida, Market Day* (54" × 64"), are the two largest known works dating from this period and the visit to Mexico (plate 119). Perhaps they were studio works executed after John's return. "He said that he was 'only ready to begin to paint' when he left Mexico after six months."[293] Further, in the same interview, it is inferred that O'Shea painted the Mexican people in watercolor "partly for variety and partly for the very practical reason that watercolors are easier to pack about than the more bulky paraphernalia of oil painting."

120

In any case, *Comida, Market Day* was hung at the Harrison Memorial Library in Carmel during the week of April 12, 1937, almost two years after the trip to Mexico began in 1935. The City acquired this painting through the Federal Art Project, funded by the Works Project Administration:

> In order to take advantage of the unprecedented opportunity to own a major art work of one of the outstanding resident artists, the city agreed, many months ago, to "sponsor" a large painting for the library. With the privilege of naming a "request" artist through the non-relief quota of their project, it was stipulated that Mr. O'Shea be engaged to do the painting.[294]

The Federal Art Project for the Monterey District was being supervised during these years by fellow artist Burton Shepard Boundey (1879–1962).[295]

Although a considerably more modest work than the earlier Netherlandish scenes, *Comida, Market Day*, in its depiction of peasants engaged in everyday activities, is reminiscent of a number of country scenes by Peter Brueghel the Elder. The busy mealtime gathering is full of symbolism—implied or revealed. Four women and eight men are busy moving toward a table, perhaps for supper. The principal male figure in white and the female figure in blue with her back to the viewer could be saying grace while the rest of the party find their places at the crowded table, eight of them looking directly at John O'Shea, beckoning him to take the ample seat of honor being reserved at the head of the table.

A vividly fluent feeling permeates the rendering of foreground, table, and clothing. As usual in this technique, more detailed, realistic strokes are necessary to emphasize specific facial features. The green-blue of the women's "mantas" responds to a thin stripe of teal blue sky over the short, tiled roof, upper left, and the terra cotta-red roof below the sky matches the shirt color of the man immediately behind the white-clad host.

To our knowledge, this is the only large group picture in oil that O'Shea ever painted—truly "a major art work."[294] Another painting of the Mexican period, entitled *Going Home from Market*, now unlocated, was said to have been purchased about 1952 by a collector for placement in the Chicago Art Institute.[7] However, that institution does not now own any work by John O'Shea.[296]

120. NATIVE CHILDREN, cat. no. 295.

Opposite page, COMIDA, MARKET DAY, *ca.* 1936, detail of plate 119.

100

121

122

121. Copy of Robert Henri's sketchbook entry for *Chow-Choy*. Note comments on "La Jolla," painting directions, History, Science and Art exhibition in 1914, and many other exhibition sites. Present whereabouts of finished painting, depicted in William Innes Homer, p. 255, is unknown. Courtesy of Janet J. LeClair, New York.

122. MEXICAN GIRL, Coll. City of Carmel-by-the-Sea, cat. no. 71.

Why Henri?

"... *Mexican 'Head', a moving face full of character and emotion. Enhanced by a white background the portrait has a religious splendor.*"

Rosalie James, *Carmel Pine Cone*, December 10, 1937.

123. HOLY MAN, *ca.* 1935, cat. no. 56.

A good many words have been written about the ancestry or lineage of Robert Henri's style of portraiture. A short pedigree would include Frans Hals, whom he "discovered" at Haarlem in 1896,[297] and whose palette darkened Henri's earlier light and Impressionist one. Understanding of the subject and the inner significance of things were features of Rembrandt's portraits which Henri sought to capture rapidly with accurate brush strokes.[298] In 1903 via Whistler, Sargent, and Chase, who "had recently popularized the full-length portrait type, and following the example of Velázquez's rendition of Spanish nobility,"[299] Henri, "whose other God was Velázquez"[300] (especially after seeing his work at the Prado in 1895), began his long series of portraits, full-length and partial figure, on dark backgrounds. To this end:

> Henri eliminated the usual props, the furniture, statuary, vases, and carpet. As in cases of some works by Manet and Velázquez, his figure exists in a shallow space devoid of background objects, compositional gimmicks and sentimentality.[301]

What precisely changed the fundamental nature of Henri's portrait style is not clear. However, two of his famous portraits herald this change. *Viv in Blue Stripe* and *Portrait of Mrs. Robert Henri* were both painted in 1914 while the Henris and Violet, Mrs. Henri's sister, were occupying "a small cottage in La Jolla [California], virtually at the ocean's edge, a dozen miles from San Diego."[302] In both instances "he eliminated the last vestiges of the dark palette"[303] and in the latter, especially, he used "a veritable symphony of hues."[304]

In September 1914, fourteen of these portraits were exhibited at the Museum of History, Science and Art in Los Angeles and elicited an excellent review.[304] As Ruth Westphal points out in *Plein Air Painters of California*, this institution, founded in 1913, incorporated the first public art gallery in Los Angeles. Presumably, as stated above, O'Shea viewed Bellows's works here in 1915.[39] There is a good chance that he also saw Henri's on this occasion. Among the works on display was the portrait of *Chow Choy, 1914*, a Chinese girl whom Henri painted in San Diego[305] (plate 121).

Although dealing with fewer known works by O'Shea than Henri, it would be difficult not to acknowledge a parallel stylistic evolution in the portraits of Henri from 1903 to 1914 and of O'Shea from 1922 to 1936. From the somber, dark palette of *Pop Hart*, *Grandma*, and *Blind Woman of Taos*, O'Shea switched to the flashing colors on light background of *The Mexican Girl* (or *Woman of Taxco?*) (plate 122), *The Mexican Man*, and even in the very serious subject of the *Holy Man*, which he depicted in three separate, distinct works—all on stark white backgrounds[306] (plate 123).

Somewhat later, in 1917 or 1918, on his second visit to Santa Fe and neighboring towns, after completing several canvases incorporating his traditionally plain background, Henri began to paint sitters in front of "brilliantly-

124

125

colored-and-patterned blankets" which "was a departure from his long-held view that a background is good in color and form when it is so certainly there that you do not think of it."[307]

Many similarities in technique and concept between the work of John O'Shea and his contemporaries seem purely coincidental until the lives and works of other artists are studied. This study inevitably leads to the conclusion that stimulation exists which profoundly and mutually influences the work of all artists—the more "established" ones as well as the newcomers to the art "scene"; the "properly trained" as well as the self-educated ones; those who have to paint for a living and those who enjoy painting and must paint, but whose livelihood does not depend upon it.

Why Henri? If one accepts the obvious similarities between many of O'Shea's canvases and those of Henri, it would not seem out of place to draw parallels between O'Shea's work and that of many other painters of his day. In addition it has been said that:

> Henri's importance to American art was by no means only in his work. His teaching helped to shape two generations of American artists. *The Immortal Eight and Its Influence*, published by the Art Students League in 1983, lists nearly 600 students who worked with Henri at the League alone. If his pupils at his own school, the Chase School, Moore College of Art, and his other teaching assignments were added in, the total number of his students would probably be several thousand. If one leafs through an edition of *Who's Who in American Art* published in the 1940s and '50s, the notation, "Studied with Robert Henri" occurs with remarkable frequency. For those not able to study with him directly, there was his book, *The Art Spirit*, published in 1923, which contained his philosophy of art and life.[308]

124. SEATED MAN, cat. no. 284.

125. MAN IN ARM CHAIR, cat. no. 274.

126. ANGRY SEA, cat. no. 2.

During the writing of this book on O'Shea's life, I have been asked the following questions by knowledgeable collectors: "Don't those two paintings (plates 13, 126) remind you of Bellows?" Bellows was a student of Henri and later taught many of Henri's students. "Doesn't the watercolor by George Luks entitled *Landscape Upstate* (*ca.* 1930)[309] remind you of O'Shea's watercolors of the Santa Cruz mountains (plates 127, 128)?" Luks, with Henri, was one of "The Eight."

There is a strong resemblance in the technique and subject matter of "Pop" Hart's watercolor, *Centaurs and Nymphs*, 1921,[309] and the technique of "laying in color" and "divisionist strokes"[43,44] discussed earlier in connection

127

128

with Norman St. Clair's work and O'Shea's Laguna Beach watercolors. Pop Hart and O'Shea were very good friends who shared experiences on the progress of painting and successes, or lack thereof, in exhibitions.[310] Hart's simple formula in life, "wander widely and make pictures,"[311] led him to many parts of the world to capture images of humanity in watercolor and prints. Some of his Mexican scenes from the late twenties have all the ingredients which O'Shea appreciated: "market places, fiestas, picnics, cock fights and outdoor bathers—scenes where ordinary people are having a good time." However, O'Shea, even in the caricatures he was fond of drawing, and in many pieces drawn from memory,[259] also depicted serious, sad, introverted moods and a certain pathos.

127. SANTA CRUZ HILLS, cat. no. 203.

128. COAST RANGE, cat. no. 139.

129. RED-BROWN HILLS, BLUE MOUNTAINS, cat. no. 195.

129

130. PORTRAIT: RED HEAD WOMAN, cat. no. 277.

131. MEXICAN, A PORTRAIT, Coll. Gyöngy Laky and Thomas Layton, San Francisco, cat. no. 70. Photograph by Ansel Adams, San Francisco.

For example, returning to the Mexican work and O'Shea's three portraits of a "holy man," Thelma B. Miller of the *Carmel Pine Cone* said:

> Best of the collection of Mexican "types" I liked the series of three of a "holy man," a cracked, fanatical soul from the depths. The first, just after the artist captured him, shows him wild, unshaven, with a glare in his eyes like that of a frightened wild animal. In the second a wistful quality emerges, and by the third, after a few weeks of regular feeding and a bit of cleaning up, the face has found its essential spirituality.[306]

One, perhaps two, of these three paintings are known today.

In a different spirit entirely is the *Mexican, A Portrait* on wooden panel (plate 131), depicting an obviously well-to-do and well-dressed man; sombrero, face, and rebozo are painted with minute brush strokes and infinite care. The painting is signed on the front and the reverse and dated 1936. It bears a sticker for a San Francisco Museum of Art Exhibition dated April 2, 1936.[312] That O'Shea ascribed some special importance to this portrait is surmised from the fact that he had at least two studio photographs made of the work—the photographer was Ansel Adams of San Francisco.

Some of O'Shea's work has been likened to that of Arthur Wesley Dow (1857–1922) and a relationship there may indeed exist since Dow taught Composition at the Art Students League from 1897 to 1903.

106

132

132. GRASSY HILLS, cat. no. 53.

133. COAST HILLS, CARMEL VALLEY, cat. no. 21.

Finally, a composition like that of *Grassy Hills* (plate 132) cannot but recall analytic realism (often somewhat gratuitously called "Cubist"), a style ascribed to many works of O'Shea's California contemporary—illustrator, painter, and muralist L. Maynard Dixon (1875–1946) after 1930.[313] As early as November 1919, Dixon, who had relatives in Carmel, was mentioned in the local press.[314] In November 1920 it was noted that his "new technique combines well-known cowboy and Indian characters with Western plains and *mountains* in a broader and entirely new way."[315] As previously noted, Dixon was among the principal artists who stimulated the creation of the Beaux Arts Galerie in San Francisco for the promotion of "contemporary art"—and O'Shea exhibited there in a one-man show in 1928. O'Shea's portrayal of mountains, desert, and sky in his paintings of the Southwest exude a feeling of vastness not unlike that depicted so well by Dixon. And, in passing, it is further noted that Dixon spent much time in Taos where he, like O'Shea, went in 1930.[316]

133

O'Shea is thought to have painted at least one mural, but it has not been located. Although it was recalled that it had been painted for the Officers' Club at Ft. Ord, California,[28] none has been located either in the old club facilities (Martinez Hall), the present club, or the Stilwell Recreation Hall; the latter building, now in considerable disrepair and practically falling into the ocean, still houses a number of interesting works by Monterey Peninsula artists of the 1930s and 1940s, but none by O'Shea.

Regardless of the comparisons that can be made between the paintings of John O'Shea and other artists, his work as a whole remains diversified but uniquely personal, often yielding only fragmentary or minimal clues to represent complex compositions, and displaying bold coloration, depth, and a feeling of instant mood.

Again, drawing a parallel between O'Shea and Henri, O'Shea showed a number of his paintings on several occasions, and Henri, according to the precise notes he maintained on every painting, entered many of his paintings in many exhibitions—sometimes several times a year.[317]

A résumé of similarities noted between Henri's and O'Shea's lives and works is presented here, for what it is worth:

ROBERT HENRI	JOHN O'SHEA
Name change from Cozad to Henri	Shea to O'Shea
Paints fluently "Impressionist" works early on	Same
Lives at Sherwood Studios, 1901–06	Same; surely 1921–22
Paints on Monhegan Island; surf, rocks, country and trees	Same, also on mainland
Paints in New Mexico	Same
Early portraits dark	Same
Later portraits light and colorful	Same
Painted "hundreds" of children	Didn't paint many, but was fond of children
Liked painting "types"	Same
Painted landscapes	Same
Painted seascapes	Same
"Only so much you can do with coastal pictures"	Same
Became Academician	No
but worked outside of that realm	Same
Repainted pictures	Same
Adored the Irish countryside and Irish people	Don't know, but had many Irish friends
Painted often rapidly "to catch the mood"	Same
Showed paintings over and over	Same
Had a compulsion to paint	Same
but had to paint for a living; also gambled	No
Pursued etching only briefly	Same
First wife had miscarriage; no children	Molly had miscarriage or child out of wedlock
Flirted with Socialism "when artists and writers were catching it right and left"	Same
Exhibited and was in Los Angeles, 1915	Same
Lived in seaside cottage at La Jolla, California, 1914	Laguna Beach, California, 1916
Was good friend of former student Alice Klauber of San Diego	Olga Epstein, a San Francisco interior designer, once tried to "place" one of O'Shea's paintings of bananas in the Fine Arts Gallery of San Diego with the help of her cousin, Alice Klauber[318]
Painted Ruth St. Denis in New York, 1919	Ruth St. Denis danced in Carmel in 1921. Lilith James (Mrs. Dan James) took dance lessons in Hollywood from St. Denis in the mid-twenties.

Inconsequential, or indeed spurious as some of these similarities may seem when considered individually, they do serve, when taken as a whole and in retrospect, to place John O'Shea in the appropriate historical milieu and to suggest his position as one of the leaders shaping the art world of his time.

134. POINT LOBOS TREES, cat. no. 86.

"I am sure that John O'Shea, in passing, notes those trees: he has a passionate sympathy with the will of a tree to thrust skyward, the will of a cliff to endure."

Ella Young, *Flowering Dusk*.

Just Before the War

135

"'One mustn't overlook the Irish twirks of humor that sometimes appear, either,' an admirer of his work points out. 'Sometimes it is of the sardonic quality and sometimes light and lyrical, but it can be found in many of his paintings.'"

Dorothy Stephenson, *Monterey Peninsula Herald*, November 1, 1946.

Opposite page, SEASCAPE, detail of plate 147.

135. BIG TREE, cat. no. 132.

Nineteen thirty-six was a busy year for John O'Shea, then approaching sixty. Besides readying the results of his Mexican trip for the spring exhibition in San Francisco and the large show encompassing the "Subjects of Mexico" at the Del Monte Gallery, he also showed *Agate Mountain*, a watercolor, at the Fall Exhibition of the San Francisco Art Association, concentrating on "Watercolors, Pastels and Tempera on Paper." *Agate Mountain* had been shown earlier that year at the Del Monte Gallery and like the oil painting *Woman of Taxco*, was priced at $500, marking it, in the opinion of the artist, as an equally valuable work.

In addition to John's busy exhibition schedule, the O'Sheas spent the winter of 1936–37 "in the East," first visiting her relatives again in Terre Haute, spending January in Florida, and ending their vacation at the St. Moritz Hotel in New York City before returning to Carmel Highlands in February.[319]

The name of John O'Shea or the O'Sheas appeared almost on a weekly basis in the *Carmel Pine Cone* during these years. There were regular monthly or bi-monthly exhibitions at the gallery of the Carmel Art Association to which O'Shea contributed one or more paintings. As a Director of the Association and after his election as President on August 9, 1937, he was involved with their business, and particularly that of planning and construction of additions to the gallery building on Dolores Street.

In April there was the Works Progress Administration presentation to the Harrison Memorial Library. In May O'Shea showed works of various subjects at the William Rockhill Nelson Gallery of Art, Atkins Museum of Fine Arts in Kansas City, Missouri;[320] twelve were returned in June.[321]

Costume parties, spirited impromtu dances in and out of costume, spontaneous recitals, beach parties, and marches down Ocean Avenue in Carmel—in the middle of the night—were among the regular entertainments indulged in by "early Carmelites" and Carmel Highlanders. Entries in Edward Weston's *Daybooks* are full of such enthusiastic affairs. When not entertaining at home or on the "Cliff Property," the O'Sheas often attended parties elsewhere. At a "big mask party" in September 1929, for instance, where could be seen "all walks of life: Pebble Beach, Highlands Society to Carmel Bohemians," Molly O'Shea appeared as a Portuguese peasant.[322]

In June 1937:

> John and Molly O'Shea were the added touch of color at the Music Society's annual jinks. . . . They appeared in colorful Seminole Indian costumes [which they probably purchased in Florida the previous winter]. Posters on the walls in keeping with the society's program were done in bold strokes by Artist O'Shea.[323]

The Carmel Art Association showed works by its members at the Stanford (University) Gallery in November and O'Shea was among "artists prominently identified as leading names in American art."[324]

136

136. RED ROCKS BY THE SEA, Coll. Gordon and Joan Spencer, cat. no. 194.

137. TRUNK, ROCK, SAND AND SEA, cat. no. 213.

138. TRUNKS AND ROUGH SEA, cat. no. 214.

The Pulitzer Prize-winning playwright and author Martin Flavin and his wife, Sarah, were good friends of Shawn and Molly O'Shea. Their home, "Spindrift,"[325] was nearby on Yankee Point at cliff's edge overlooking the Pacific. This "substantial residence" was built during 1921–22 at a cost of $50,000 and was occupied in May 1922. At that time it was "the house farthest south (from Carmel) at Yankee Point, but other houses are planned."[326] *Spindrift* was also the title of a Flavin play that premiered at the Pasadena Playhouse in April 1930.[327] The home, now on Spindrift Road, subsequently provided scenes for the movie *Rebecca*.[325]

Parties at O'Shea's "Cliff Property," which often included the Flavins, were frequently documented in photographs, and Martin sat for a large portrait in the late thirties. John painted a watercolor sketch of a redwood bar located between greenery, which he inscribed to Martin Flavin on a birthday, and on one occasion at "Spindrift," John, who had been drinking excessively and became more abusive to Molly than could be tolerated by the rest of the party, was asked by the host to leave and go home.[328]

137

Sarah Flavin's body, "claimed by the sea" near "Spindrift" early in December 1937, was found off the rocks on January 5, 1938. Upon her tragic disappearance, Flavin first called on his neighbor John O'Shea.[329]

Eventually Martin Flavin moved to an attractive Pebble Beach house, a remodeled stable[325] formerly the studio and workshop of sculptor and painter Joseph (Jo) Jacinto Mora (1876–1947).

The frequent Carmel Art Association Gallery exhibitions continued throughout 1938. In February the Association, sponsored by a number of service organizations in Salinas, the Monterey County seat, presented the first exhibition of works by its artists in that city. In May the exhibition at the Carmel Art Gallery was "bannered as the best watercolor show [the Gallery] has yet hung . . . interjected are two striking John O'Shea paintings in gesso."[330] According to San Francisco artist John Langley Howard, watercolor medium is not commonly used on gesso because of rapid loss of porosity, but Howard

"He has caught on his canvas the weight of a bough; the impatient frustrated surge of the sea; the very muscle and texture of rocks."

Ella Young, *Flowering Dusk*.

138

139. SEASCAPE AND ROCKS, *ca.* 1939, cat. no. 99.

suggested that "O'Shea's rapid method of painting on a large scale" could have allowed for this unusual combination, otherwise unknown in O'Shea's work.[331] Coincidentally, Howard was living in Carmel in 1938 and also showed at this exhibition; his was a "fine fish wharf scene in modern manner, which is good waterfront characterization and animated."[330] The work is known today.

John O'Shea was re-elected unanimously to his second term as President of the Association in August, and the same month the *Carmel Pine Cone* proclaimed: "O'Shea Dominant in Art Gallery August Exhibit."[332] Is there any wonder that someone should have written the poem we presented earlier (on page 34)—"The Ritschel, The Hansen and The Great O'Shea"—first published on September 23, 1938?

141

140

140. A marker on Seventeen Mile Drive in Pebble Beach indicates where "The Witch Cypress," a gnarled tree, stood until overturned by the wind in 1964. In the late 1930s the O'Sheas occupied this house across the street from the landmark (bottom). A view of the shore at this location, 1984, includes large boulders. Water, gnarled trees, and boulders were the subject of many of O'Shea's works, especially in black and white and mixed media.

141. ROCK PEAKS AND SURF, cat. no. 199.

As can best be determined Molly and Shawn O'Shea left their spacious home in Carmel Highlands in 1938–39 and moved to Pebble Beach (plate 140). The O'Sheas' place, remembered fondly by a few today, had "a magnificent, large baronial living room all done in a lavish Spanish style"[333] and an unobstructed view of the Pacific—unfortunately obstructed today by overgrown trees. Eventually, the Carmel–San Simeon Highway was completed, and when it opened in March 1937,[334] automobile traffic began moving just a stone's throw east of the house and the entrance to their property.

A quarter of a century had passed since the 1913 Armory Show in New York and O'Shea's arrival in California. Whether he personally visited the two great painting exhibitions of 1915–16 in San Diego and San Francisco or the 1935 exhibition in San Diego is not known. During these years O'Shea had traveled extensively and had exhibited many works in dozens of shows from New York City to Los Angeles and Tucson to Sacramento; not only one-man shows, but group shows that brought him together with many other artists. His cosmopolitan, inquisitive nature and his wide circle of friends would surely bring him into contact with ideas generated by these three major events and others—ideas concerning both painting specifically and broader trends in art and art philosophy.

A constant flow of favorable press reviews and commentaries on his work must have been not only very gratifying, but self-assuring, and no signs of imminent deterioration of artistic achievement were apparent. In retrospect, however, changes—very profound ones—were soon to occur, in all likelihood instigated more by international political events than by any predictable, gradual, or even eruptive evolution of art itself. The world was at peace on February 18, 1939, when the Golden Gate International Exposition opened on Treasure Island in the Bay of San Francisco. After being extended to the following year, it finally closed on September 29, 1940. By this time World War II was raging in Europe and was soon to engulf North Africa, the Pacific, the Far East, and Asia and would, of course, involve the United States in 1941.

142

142. OLD TRUNKS, cat. no. 172.

143. SEA RHYTHM, *ca.* 1939, cat. no. 98.

An interesting résumé of this situation vis-à-vis art, as seen in retrospect, follows:

> Art hit the headlines in 1939 at the Golden Gate International Exposition on Treasure Island in San Francisco Bay. The Exposition brought an outstanding collection of European contemporary paintings to the Bay Area and also featured a significant exhibition of the work of many living California artists. Not since the Panama-Pacific International Exposition in 1915 had Northern California enjoyed an art exhibition of equal size and quality. The Treasure Island art exhibitions were planned to stimulate the growth of art on the West Coast; but their organizers could not have foreseen that World War II would bring changes which would cause us to view the Exposition more as an endpoint than a beginning. Treasure Island's chief significance for California painting is, in fact, that it was a culmination of art between the wars and a convenient milestone by which this art can be judged in relation to its international contemporaries.
>
> The Exposition on Treasure Island is most remembered for its massive outdoor monuments to Pacific Basin cultures. Its murals, sculptures, lights, and architecture drew praise and delighted visitors in the exotic "Magic City" they created. The Executive Committee for the Fair was committed to patronizing California artists for these works and the art press proclaimed the fairgrounds impressive testimony to local talent.
>
> The painting exhibitions at the Exposition are probably less remembered, but are of equal interest for the history of California painting. For local artists, Treasure Island was a rare opportunity to show their work before an international audience and for many it coincided with the peaks of their careers. Two separate exhibitions featured California painters: the large Contemporary American Exhibition in the Palace of Fine Arts and the more modest State-sponsored exhibition of California art in the California State Building—both on Treasure Island. Together, these exhibitions reveal much about the nature of contemporary painting in California in 1939.[335]

It is debatable in which of the two separate exhibitions showing simultaneously on Treasure Island in 1939 it was better to have been a part. Both had their respective political supporters, but each gave wide exposure to the works of scores of artists. To reiterate, two separate exhibitions featured California painters: the large Contemporary American Exhibition in the Palace of Fine Arts (built to be used as an airplane hangar later) and the more modest state-sponsored exhibition of California art in the California State Building.

For O'Shea at the beginning of 1939, it would appear that his interest in his art and its promotion remained undaunted. By invitation or by design, the artist, now listed as living in Pebble Beach, showed *Tahitian Bananas* in the California State Building on Treasure Island from February to December; *Superstition Mountains* at the State Fair in Sacramento, September 1–10; and *Early Spring; Old Trees, Monterey* and *Mexican Girl* at the Oakland Art Gallery. The latter exhibition was with Artist Members of the Bay Region Art Association, November to December.

That he also found time to paint during 1939 is assumed from the date of the oil painting *Monterey Cypress* in the Collection of the Sheldon Swope Art Gallery, Terre Haute, Indiana, since 1979. More recently Robert D. Kinsman wrote:

> O'Shea traveled extensively and assimilated a variety of influences into a personal style distinguished by bold shapes, creamy textures and vivid color. In its blue, green, orange and ochre palette; uniform density of light, atmosphere and color saturation; and color patch construction, "A Monterey Cypress" reflects the influence of the great French Post-Impressionist master, Paul Cézanne. Cézanne, Vincent van Gogh, and other Post-Impressionists borrowed from Japanese printmakers the practice of viewing the scene from above and the motif of a cropped foreground object (the tree here) raking diagonally across the picture plane. All of these elements appear in "A Monterey Cypress," but are handled with imagination and verve by O'Shea.[336]

The Golden Gate International Exposition was extended into 1940 and that year O'Shea showed another painting, again in the California Building. *Sea Rhythm* (more recently erroneously titled *Maine Sea*), a large and dramatic work (plate 143), is depicted in an *Illustrated Catalogue* of the 1940 portion of the exhibition, dedicated to "Illustrations of Works of Committee and Jury Members." Ferdinand Burgdorff, Paul Dougherty, N.A., Arthur Hill Gilbert, A.N.A., John O'Shea, Armin Hansen, N.A., and Myron Oliver constituted the Monterey Bay District Committee and Jury of Selection under Chairman William Ritschel, N.A. The chairman of the Advisory Committee for the entire affair was writer, critic, "flamboyant personality," and controversial professor of art at the University of California at Berkeley, "the Prussian know-all" and painter, and "a devotee of Impressionism," (Karl) Eugen Neuhaus (1879–1963).[337]

144. PORTRAIT; WHITE-HAIRED MAN, cat. no. 187.

145. CYPRESS TRUNKS AND FOREST, cat. no. 146.

146. PORTRAIT; WOMAN IN BLACK, cat. no. 189.

147. SEASCAPE, cat. no. 206.

145

144

Agate Mountain, shown in 1936, was shown once more in 1940 at the Del Monte Gallery at a watercolor exhibition and was praised as one of "other fine examples of O'Shea's art."[338] This event was headlined "Group Exhibits by O'Shea and Boundey At Del Monte Gallery Win Admiration." Burton Shepard Boundey visited and was "keen about Carmel" in 1923;[339] he settled in Monterey in 1926.[295] Boundey had been a student of Robert Henri and George Wesley Bellows, among other teachers. This was the last exhibition held at the famous Del Monte Gallery,[295] which had opened in 1907.[340] Josephine Mildred Blanch wrote eloquently about the Del Monte Gallery in 1914:

> When the history of California art is written, Monterey Peninsula will furnish a colorful and important chapter and the Del Monte Gallery will be recognized as a large factor in the development of art in the State.

O'Shea had not been in Northern California in 1907, but now at the Del Monte Gallery's closing Miss Blanch wrote:

> In fact, the facility with which O'Shea handles this flowing intractible medium, at the same time preserving richness of color and losing nothing in texture and characterization, is a marvel to one who studies his art critically.[338]

A noteworthy reminiscence by Burton Boundey, who knew both Henri and O'Shea well, was received recently. It recalled that:

> John O'Shea was one of our very *fine* painters. Whether in landscapes or portraits, he strove for *character* . . . casting aside all that seemed unimportant. Robert Henri's favorite word, "integrity," would have applied to O'Shea. I twice had the honor of holding two-man shows with him. And sometimes he was a law unto himself. When invited by Dayton, Ohio, Art Institute to hold a one-man show, he asked me to let him include one of *my* paintings. Apparently it worked out all right for later I received a very nice letter from the curator of the gallery. O'Shea's work had the respect of the best painters, and he was often asked to serve on important juries.[341]

"*To the observer, O'Shea is primal rather than primitive. He sweeps aside not-essentials, even those that have gained the assent of centuries. But he accepts values.*"

Robert H. Wilson for the *San Francisco Bulletin*, quoted in *The Carmelite*, April 11, 1928.

147

A final comment on this exhibition: a watercolor entitled *Land of A Thousand Smokes* (entry no. 9) is said by Miss Blanch in her review to be "a landscape of an Alaskan subject." We do not know if, or when, O'Shea was in Alaska, but it could have been in connection with one of his sea voyages to either the South Pacific or Hawaii.[538]

At year's end O'Shea was again exhibiting at the Oakland Art Gallery: *The Pali* representing his Hawaiian period and *Taos Landscape*, his New Mexican.

146

Bohemian Once More

Nineteen hundred forty-one was a sad year for John O'Shea. In early summer, on a beautiful site by the ocean in Pebble Beach, his wife and campanion for nearly thirty years showed signs of grave illness. Molly was admitted to St. Luke's Hospital in San Francisco in August and died of cancer on October 7, 1941.

Noël Sullivan, their friend and the one who had laid the ground work for Shawn's major exhibition at the Legion of Honor in San Francisco, wrote a long and thought-provoking tribute to Molly. From it we gather that "her deepest preoccupation was with the eternal values and the unending life of the spirit."[342]

A month earlier O'Shea's oil painting *Rusty Cypress* (no. 41) was awarded first prize in the Decorative Class at the Eighty-sixth Annual Exhibition of Paintings at the California State Fair in Sacramento; the second and third prizes went to Paul Dougherty, N.A., of Carmel, and Nicholas P. ("Nick") Brigante (b. 1895), a Southern California artist and member of the group of Independent Artists in Los Angeles.[10, 343] For a reasonable guess of the approximate monetary value of this prize, in the previous year, William Ritschel, N.A., had won first prize of sixty dollars in the Marines Class for his entry, *Song of the Sea*.

148. CYPRESS TRUNK, cat. no. 288.

149. POISED, cat. no. 177.

150

150. Bohemian Club members and friends, at "The Grove," 1941. Shown at the Campfire Circle are: (left to right, top to bottom) Cloyd Sweigert, Artist, Cartoonist; Matteo Sandona, Artist; Rene Weaver, Artist; Ferdinand Burgdorff, Artist; Albert J. Camille, Art Director; Arthur Cahill, Artist; Dohrman H. Smith, Advertising Cartoonist; John O'Shea; Eustace Cullinan, Lawyer; Unidentified (light jacket); Francis Todhunter, Artist; Bernard Maybeck, Architect; E. Spencer Macky, Artist, Teacher; Maurice Logan, Artist. Identification courtesy of Club members: Dr. Andrew G. Jameson, Dr. Charles A. Rowe, Mr. Charles F. Bulotti, Mr. Paul T. Carey (1985). Photograph by Gabriel Moulin, San Francisco.

O'Shea became an artist-member of San Francisco's Bohemian Club in 1941, as noted in the Club's records. A number of photographs exist of John O'Shea and fellow artists at the Club's encampment at "The Grove," taken by the official photographer Gabriel Moulin in fall of 1941 (plate 150). Also recorded by Moulin is what appears to be a large framed charcoal, crayon, or watercolor poster, signed John O'Shea, attached to a redwood tree and depicting a number of men encircling huge redwood trees with their backs to the viewer. On the work appears the title: *The Urination of Care*.

The Society for Sanity in Art, originally organized in the late 1930s in Chicago, had by 1941 established a branch in San Francisco.[344] The group eventually evolved into the Society of Western Artists. Considered by some to be "one of the more pathetic and yet fascinating manifestations of violently anti-modern sentiment,"[345] the Society, nevertheless, counted a large number of prominent painters among its members. John O'Shea, not one to be easily influenced by voguish trends in art, showed *The Stream*, an oil painting unlocated today, at the Society's exhibition at the California Palace of the Legion of Honor, November 1941–January 1942.

151

That John missed Molly this first Christmas season without her is reflected in a letter he wrote two years later to her sister:

> How dearest Molly in her great wisdom and goodness made this season and always a good world to live in. What an occasion Xmas was to her! And what an outpouring of heart and energy! God bless her dear Spirit!
>
> And what great beauty went into each and every gift at this season.
>
> If there be or be not a survival most surely his radiant goodness survives in us and enriches us and ascends with us and makes us better for us and blessed in having the rich gifts of his inexhaustible spirit.[346]

Happily John O'Shea's spirits and artistic motivation were strong enough to sustain his interest in painting. Alfred Frankenstein, writer, music and art critic, and lecturer, wrote in the *San Francisco Chronicle* after viewing the March 1942 exhibition of paintings at the Bohemian Club:

> Several new artist members have recently been admitted to membership [in the Bohemian Club] and the Club's annual exhibition now on view is greatly improved thereby. [He tells about Jules Pages and William Gaw] . . . John O'Shea's landscapes and still lifes are exceptionally brilliant in color and interesting in their play of half-abstracted forms.[347]

Richard L. Masten, playwright and onetime owner-editor of the *Carmel Pine Cone* and *Cymbal*, had moved in February 1928 to an elegant villa built on a cliff at the eastern limit of Wild Creek Canyon in the Highlands. In 1937 he moved to Sausalito, California.[348] The widower John O'Shea moved from Pebble Beach back to Carmel Highlands in 1942 and occupied the "Masten House"[28,64] (plate 153). Undoubtedly a number of watercolors and oil paintings were created from this vantage point overlooking the ocean, surf, and rocks beyond the inlet surrounded by steep cliffs. A spectrum of colors, from the dark blue of the deeper ocean to the turquoise green of the shallow waters, from the bright white of the surf to the crashing of waves on black-brown-reddish rocks, can be seen there on sunny days (plates 154, 155).

"His 'Dahlias' is a pyramid of glory in form and color."
Thelma B. Miller, *Carmel Pine Cone*, September 10, 1937.

151. DAHLIAS, *ca.* 1920, Coll. Molly Jeppson, cat. no. 33.

152. FAR MOUNTAINS, cat. no. 42.

152

John entertained here also. Richard Criley, Theodore Criley's son, living then in Chicago, but who came to Carmel Highlands on annual visits to see his widowed mother, remembers many gatherings there.

On one such occasion, John's temper as well as his impatience flared with a telephone caller who asked over and over again for directions to John's house as he wished to purchase a painting. Finally exasperated, John was heard to say: "No, the way you are headed will take you to Los Angeles, and that is obviously where you belong. Good-bye!"[349]

Probably toward the end of his sojourn in the "Masten House," O'Shea painted a life-size watercolor portrait of Ella Young, Shawn and Molly's longtime friend. As best we can tell, this was in 1943.[350] The painting is said to have been exhibited some years later at the Grand Central Galleries in New York,[351] but a record of this occurrence cannot be found.[352] Also, it has been stated repeatedly[28] that the portrait was intended to be used in a forthcoming book by Ella Young, but she was not happy with it. When last known the portrait had been presented to the Huntington Library in San Marino, but there is no record of this portrait at the library, only a photo—perhaps a copy of the one mentioned below. Ella Young *did* present copies of a number of her books and manuscripts to the library, and if they had ever received her portrait, they "would not have disposed of such a thing."[353] The painting remains unlocated.

153. John O'Shea's home, the "Masten House" at Wild Cat Canyon, *ca.* 1943.

154. BLUE POOL, cat. no. 13.

155. DARK ROCKS, anonymous collector, cat. no. 34.

154

155

156. PORTRAIT: ELLA YOUNG, cat. no. 512, currently unlocated. From a print, photographer unknown.

157. RED ROCKS, cat. no. 255.

156

Altogether a sad ending to a well-known portrait of a well-known poetess about which an equally well-known artist and teacher in Carmel, Patricia Cunningham, once wrote: "With equal skill he presents the personalities of his portraits. Ella Young's blue eyes in the watercolor portrait of her speak vividly of the mystic beauty of the world she lives in."[354] Fortunately photographs which O'Shea had made of the portrait still exist (plate 156). The image portrayed is similar to that of another photograph of Ella Young, taken with John in front of the latter's Pebble Beach home a year or two earlier.

At the time Ella Young received the photograph of her portrait from John, she wrote to his sister-in-law, Emma Pine, in January 1944: "He [John] is brown and strong-looking, says he climbs hillsides and is much in the open air." She goes on to say that: "he wants to get a smaller and simpler house—the one he has is cold and the roof leaks."[350] There exists an undated bill in which John itemizes various repairs "Relating to Highland Property" including "Repair to house—new door and new roof labor . . . $37 plus $171." These problems certainly provide several possible reasons for a move away from the "Masten House."

John continued serving the Carmel Art Association as Director for many years, as well as being elected second and then third Vice President for the years 1942–44.[86] He showed occasionally at Carmel, and in January–February 1943, at Santa Cruz's Fourteenth Annual Statewide Art Exhibition, he showed *Suspiring Sea*, a watercolor.

Probably John O'Shea's last major exhibition was a "Top Flight Art Show In Carmel" in June 1945. A large collection of his drawings was displayed here coincident with photographs by Edward P. McMurtry. Irene Alexander of the *Monterey Peninsula Herald*, a longtime acquaintance of and participant in the arts of the Monterey Peninsula, particularly Carmel, as well as other American cities, accorded not only that display a glowing review, but to John O'Shea, the artist, a magnificent tribute:

> Perhaps no other local artist possesses greater technical facility in handling a number of different media than O'Shea. Where some are content to go on year after year repeating a success they have attained in one field, O'Shea is continually seeking new expressions and developing his means of expression. His work is characterized not only by its spontaneity, but by the technical expertness which he displays, whatever his approach.[291]

157

128

"... in the present collection are to be found varying studies of the same tree, each new, each fresh and vital, each motivated by the artist's never-ending contemplation of his subject."
Irene Alexander, *Monterey Peninsula Herald*, June 15, 1945.

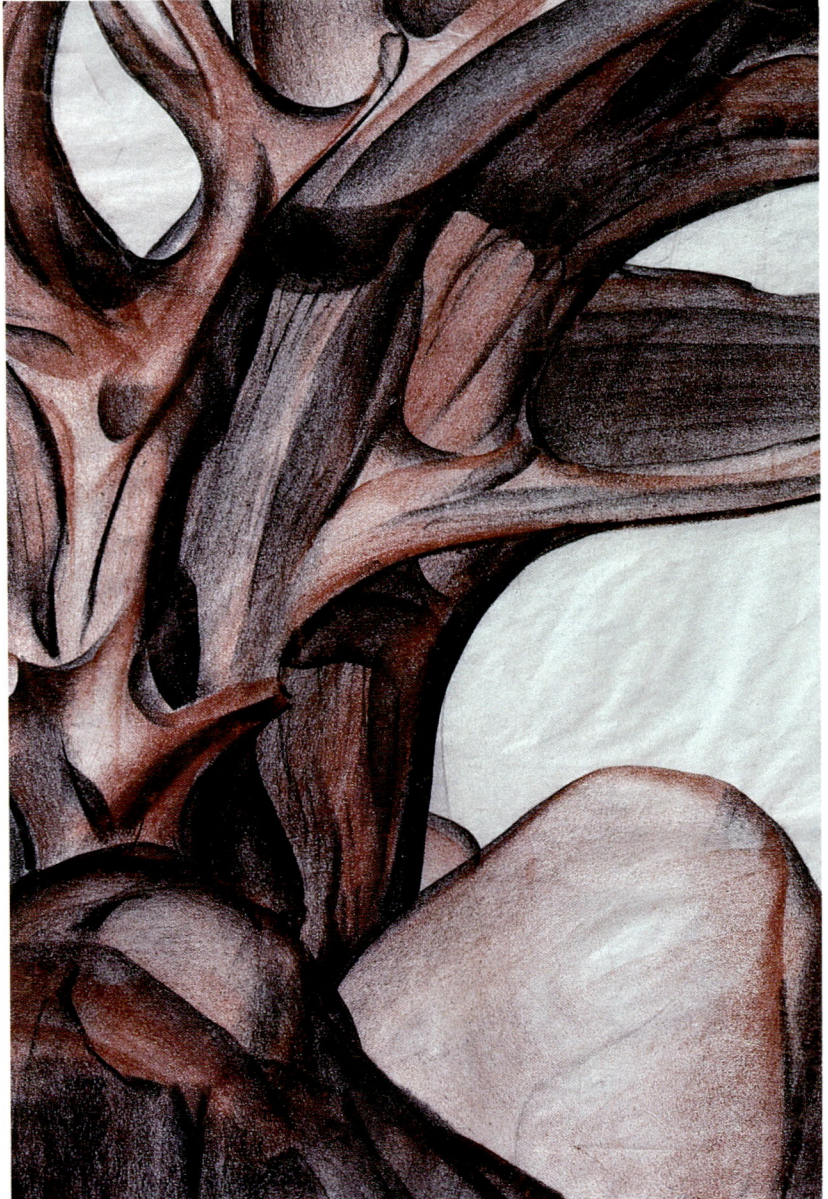
158

158. LONELY TREE, cat. no. 264.

Opposite page, FAR MOUNTAINS, detail of plate 152.

This critique also offers the only known indication of O'Shea's work with wood-block printing. As we shall see, he engaged at this time, we believe, in producing etchings as well. Concerning the woodblock Irene Alexander writes:

There is a delicacy and a whimsical symbolism in the colored wood block print entitled "Spring" . . .

"American Art Week, noted by proclamation of governors and mayors throughout the land, and celebrated from November 1–7, was inaugurated in 1928 by the Oregon chapter of the American Artist's Professional League, of which the Carmel Art Association had been an affiliate"[355] since November 5, 1941.[86] In November 1946, to celebrate American Art Week, the *Monterey Peninsula Herald* commenced a yearly Art Edition in cooperation with Peninsula merchants to pay tribute to members of the Carmel Art Association by displaying selected paintings by their members. In later years works by other artists' organizations and individuals were honored in this manner.

Collections of John O'Shea's works were thus displayed in various commercial establishments during Art Week over the next years: Betty Brickman, milliner, Monterey, 1946; Rudolph's, furniture store, Monterey, 1947; J. C. Penney Company, Monterey, 1948; and in a "local gallery," presumably the Carmel Art Association, 1950. No entry was noted for 1949. The first three of the Art Editions carried large reproductions of paintings by O'Shea: *Hawaiian Landscape*, probably an oil, in 1946; *Coast Fog*, oil, in 1947 (known today as *Big Sur Coast* and owned by Mrs. Warren M. Hussey, Terre Haute, Indiana), and *Marine*, oil, in 1948 (known today as *Down the Coast*, plate 26).[356]

130

159

Farewell to the Highlands

160

159. IN THE WOODS, cat. no. 165.

160. Residence at San Carlos Avenue and Vista in Carmel Woods, John O'Shea's last home. Photograph, 1984.

In 1944–45, John O'Shea left the "Masten House" near his beloved ocean, and moved for the last time. He purchased a bungalow on a slope at San Carlos Avenue and Vista in Carmel Woods[28] (plate 160), in a tract of homes planned in 1922, north of Carmel and contiguous with it, where homes would "conform"[357] to those of Carmel-by-the-Sea. A number of his paintings were stored on the ground floor; he did some painting in the living room and supervised the building of raised garden beds, stone patios, and walls around the house. Intermittently, Mrs. Emma Pine, Molly's sister, visited and in later years they corresponded regularly.

In Carmel Woods, John O'Shea, possibly for the first time in his life, could indulge his fondness for children. They came and went daily, usually after leaving the school one block away, and it was through the children that John became acquainted with a number of families in the neighborhood. He could walk to Ocean Avenue, Carmel's main street, and often did so to shop or eat at nearby restaurants and then took a cab home. Hansel and Gretel candies and chocolates were as popular then as now—he would buy them by the bagfuls to give to his young friends.

The Layton family were neighbors and among his acquaintances then. Dr. Walter B. Layton became O'Shea's physician, and the Layton children grew very fond of John. Emma-Rose Layton was stunned one day when her young daughter Kathy came home with oranges. She had not yet heard of John O'Shea but was familiar with "Mr. O'Shea and the Leprechaun," a popular comic strip. It took some explaining to convince her that a real and generous Mr. O'Shea had moved close by. Young Thomas Layton, like "Rickie" Criley many years earlier, was fascinated with O'Shea's welcome of him almost on the level of an adult. Thomas was intrigued with John's art and on at least one occasion was beckoned to "go ahead, take a brush and add to the painting on the easel." It would be interesting *and* amusing to know which of O'Shea's paintings had been "added to" by young Layton.

Artist-members of San Francisco's Bohemian Club celebrated *75 Years of Bohemian Art* during the first two weeks of May 1947. As indicated earlier (page 40), John O'Shea exhibited there (number 9) and subsequently donated to the Club, the portrait he had painted in New York City in 1922 of his friend and fellow artist George Overbury "Pop" Hart. Hart's own work was not unknown to Californians, and he showed in the *Modern French and American Exhibition* at the Oakland Art Gallery, October to November 1927.[358] He was primarily an etcher and lithographer but also painted in oil and watercolor. A fairly extensive exhibition and sale of Hart's works was held in May 1984 at the Bethesda Art Gallery in Maryland.[311] From viewing those works and also a large watercolor, *Centaurs and Nymphs*, 1921, in the Hirshhorn Museum collection,[309] one gets the distinct feeling that O'Shea knew "Pop" Hart's work well and was akin to it in mode of expression, particularly in the caricatures

161

and scenes of everyday Mexican life which Hart painted so often. In John O'Shea's estate there remained a Hart lithograph entitled *Springtime in New Orleans*, a copy of which was shown at the Bethesda Art Gallery and depicted in their brochure. O'Shea's print was a present from Hart and was dedicated "To a damn good Painter from his friend Pop Hart" (plate 179). The letter of transmittal, also extant, is dated May 10, 1924.[359]

Although John O'Shea continued to exhibit paintings for several more years, it was recently recalled that from 1948 on "it was not possible to get him motivated to paint again," nor was it known "when he last produced a painting."[360]

John O'Shea began to have medical problems involving heart and circulation deficiencies. He wrote to his sister-in-law about the side effects of these conditions, which involved swelling of his legs necessitating the use of rubber stockings and migraine headaches impeding his vision when writing for long periods of time. These ailments led to a progressively increasing need for medication, in O'Shea's own words somewhat later, "so I am proceeding with a new augmentation of pills—pink, red, turquoise, yellow and gray—symphonic at least!"[361] Because O'Shea had apparently stopped painting, it is interesting to read continuing accounts of new exhibitions to which he lent paintings.

Yet another new experience for him must have been membership in "The New Group." This association of artists, founded in 1951, and currently being studied and reassessed with new interest in Monterey,[362] "was established as an artists' cooperative to show new work being done in Monterey, Carmel and the Big Sur" and to exhibit works of "Klee, Picasso and Miró, to name a few." For the first exhibition of their works this ambitious "Group" met at the studio of the Malcolm Millards in Carmel Highlands, and on June 1, 1951, opened their "Art Gallery with Modern Slant in Monterey." It is characteristic of John O'Shea's work that it could elicit the following comment by Erica Franke in her description of the first joint exhibition by "The Group":

> an abstraction by Ellwood Graham and a profoundly realistic seascape by John O'Shea hung in the same room in perfect harmony.[363]

161. POINT LOBOS (Turquoise pool), cat. no. 176.

162. FURIOUS SURF, cat. no. 47.

While we have seen a good many of O'Shea's seascapes, we cannot agree that they are "profoundly realistic." In fact, regarding sea and landscapes we have in many instances been struck with:

> a subject so reduced by . . . artistic shorthand that the skill of his paint handling becomes more important than the subject.[364]

These words refer to *Rainstorm Wyoming Valley* and *Landscape at Black Walnut, Pennsylvania*, both painted by Robert Henri in 1902. It could apply equally to his *Rolling Sea*, 1903, painted on Monhegan Island,[365] and to many of O'Shea's land and seascapes as well. On the other hand, joining Rick Deragon, Registrar/Curator of the Monterey Peninsula Museum of Art, in his opinion of O'Shea seascapes he recently viewed, we would agree that "that man could really paint water, and I've seen a lot of marines!"

133

162

163

Speaking of marines, a recent conversation with Emma-Rose Layton comes to mind. Persons familiar with the Atlantic as well as the Pacific Coast shorelines, and who are also familiar with paintings thereof, can usually differentiate seascapes from these two locales. In this regard, Emma-Rose Layton told of an occasion she had about 1947 to choose from a collection of eight or ten of John O'Shea's marines which he had set out for her. She chose one and at once O'Shea remarked that only it was of the Pacific, the rest were of Atlantic waters. Ella Young also remarked on this subject in a letter to John O'Shea two years earlier. She had noticed the color of the water while driving along the coast road on her way home to Oceano, California, after visiting with John in Carmel and wrote:

> I have never seen such wonderful colour on the sea. I notice that colour on the Pacific seems to be thickly and almost solidly on the surface, as you have painted it in several of your pictures, whereas on the Atlantic, as I saw it in Ireland, colour is more translucent, more water like.[366]

By 1953, except perhaps for an occasional work being shown in group exhibitions at Carmel, John O'Shea showed paintings with less frequency.

A label attached to *A Girl Eating* indicates that it was at the James Vigeveno Galleries in Los Angeles in 1953. As an aside, Vigeveno had represented Everett Shinn, one of "The Eight," from 1943 to 1948—Shinn did mostly clown paintings for Vigeveno because he "could move a lot of them."[367] With *A Girl Eating* (plate 164), John O'Shea also added to the "High Standard Maintained in New Show at Carmel Art Association Gallery" in March 1955 when he returned "after too long absence from the gallery exhibits with [this] one of his vigorous, distinctive charcoal drawings."[368]

As previously mentioned, Rose and Seth Ulman were friends of John O'Shea. Seth, or "Mister Empire Bilder" [sic] as he was once characterized,[369] a very successful realtor, died in 1955 shortly after settling all of O'Shea's real estate business. Rose, now a successful realtor herself, who lives and transacts business in Carmel Highlands, dined on occasion with John after her husband's death. "John was a lift to many people," said Rose Ulman recently. "He never

164

165

135

163. POISED NO. 2, cat. no. 178.

164. A GIRL EATING, cat. no. 232.

165. CLOSING HOUR, cat. no. 270.

166. HEADS, cat. no. 263.

166

167

167. DEEP CHASM, cat. no. 271.

168. STILLWATER COVE, an etching, cat. no. 305.

ran after women—they ran after him! He never lost his collegiate walk." She recalled two incidents involving her, Seth, and John O'Shea that demonstrate both a playful and a serious side of John. Seth and John, it seems, were invited to a large party at Elizabeth Bigelow's house. Although Elizabeth was a notorious teetotaler, all guests got "snockered" after these two friends, equally notorious drinkers, spiked the punch heavily. The second incident was an occasion at Gallatin Powers's restaurant, the "Grub and Grog," in Bixby, down the coast from Carmel. Powers, incidentally, was the son of painter Jane Gallatin (d. 1944) of Sacramento, the wife of early Carmel developer Frank H. Powers.[370] Arriving on time for a party were Rose, Michael and Jane Foster, and Charles Sawyer. Seth and John arrived late after stopping to have a drink en route. During dinner, Sawyer, a developer, taunted John: "I'd jump off a cliff if all I could do was sit around and paint." John put down his eating utensils, met Sawyer's eyes and quietly replied, "Why don't you!"

Among John O'Shea's last artistic endeavors, in addition to the previously mentioned wood-block printing, is thought to be a series of etchings which he presumably did after moving to Carmel Woods, 1944–45.[28] Many of O'Shea's contemporaries etched; perhaps foremost among these artists was Armin Hansen, who did a long series of magnificent etchings—currently being researched for a catalogue raisonné.[371] Ritschel did a lesser number and so did August François Gay (1891–1949), a member of Oakland's Society of Six, who after leaving the San Francisco Bay Area lived first in Monterey and later in Carmel Woods near John O'Shea, where he died. Of the eight O'Shea etchings known, one depicts a Mexican village, three are of Carmel coast scenes (plates 168, 169) and four of trees. Etching, compared to *plein air* painting, would appear to be a rewarding indoor substitute for an artist once accustomed, when he was able, to strenuous physical activity in pursuit of "subject matter."

168

169

169. LOBOS, an etching, cat. no. 301.

170. Clay bust of John O'Shea, possibly by himself, early 1940s, unlocated. From a print, photographer unknown.

John O'Shea died on April 29, 1956, in his studio home at San Carlos and Vista in Carmel Woods.[372] He had suffered for years with angina pectoris, which became increasingly severe and culminated in heart failure. The funeral took place on May 4 in the Little Chapel-by-the-Sea Crematorium in Pacific Grove, California, with the Reverend Angus Dunn, Jr., Rector of All Saints Episcopal Church of Carmel, officiating. The Paul Mortuary of Pacific Grove was in charge of the funeral services, which were attended by his colleagues and friends on the Monterey Peninsula and by his sister-in-law, Emma, Mrs. Benjamin H. Pine, who, although she had visited him several times since Molly's death in 1941, was living in Terre Haute at the time.

"John O'Shea, Nationally Known Artist Dies in Carmel" was the headline in the *Monterey Peninsula Herald* the day after he died, and he was eulogized as "one of Carmel's most distinguished artists" in the *Carmel Pine Cone-Cymbal*.[373]

It is a curious fact that Emma L. Pine, the informant cited on the Certificate of Death received by the local registrar on May 3, lists the deceased as John Garret O'Shea. Save for two instances, recorded 1911–13 in New York

170

"Mr. O'Shea is a man to watch. I predict for him a bright future."

Everett C. Maxwell, *Graphic*, December 20, 1913.

(page 14), when he listed "G" as a middle initial, he did not, to our knowledge, use a middle name during his life nor was he given one when baptized; one recalls that then his name was merely John Shea.

An explanation for this latter-day appellation may be found in the fact that John O'Shea's sister, Alice Devine, addressed letters to him as John J. O'Shea in the 1940s and that her son, John J. Devine, did the same in the mid-1950s. One of these letters to O'Shea arrived after his death and was forwarded to Mrs. Pine.[374]

Yet, O'Shea's dedication of one of his handsome tree and rock drawings to his godson and namesake reads: "John O'Shea to John Garrett Williams, May 26, 1941"—indicating that he himself was not using the middle name "Garrett" (or Jarrett). Nevertheless, "Garrett" was added by a different hand to John's previously mentioned autobiographical sketch found in a family Bible. Mrs. Pine, perhaps knowing otherwise, may have put it there or alternately found it there and used it when reporting John O'Shea's death.

A recapitulation of the artist's names thus leads from John Shea on the Baptismal Certificate to John O'Shea to John G. O'Shea to John J. O'Shea to John Garrett O'Shea to finally John Garret O'Shea on the Certificate of Death. One surmises that artist John O'Shea rests in peace regardless of what one chose to call him.

140

171

Epilogue

Following his death in 1956, a memorial exhibition of twenty-nine works under the curatorship of his sometime pupil, friend, and colleague Richard Morrison Lofton (1908–1966), was accorded John O'Shea at the Carmel Art Association. An excerpt from a letter from Lofton to Emma Pine after the show seems a fitting tribute to the painter:

> I have never heard a show talked of as much in Carmel as this one. Especially among the painters.[375]

Many of O'Shea's works remained unsigned at his death. Emma Pine gave away a number of paintings and intended to sell the remainder. In 1960 she had a document prepared, a copy of which was to accompany the unsigned works. A facsimile of this document is presented on page 174.

Three years later, the Laky Galleries in Carmel initiated a series of exhibitions and sales of O'Shea's works which lasted until 1967. Thereafter, the name and works of John O'Shea were largely overshadowed by those of younger artists and newcomers to the Monterey Peninsula.

"... 'You didn't expect me to treat the grandeur of the desert mountains the same as I would a pastoral scene, did you? What I have painted is what the desert gave me.'"

Carmel Pine Cone, May 18, 1928.

171. CYPRESSES AND TURQUOISE SKY, cat. no. 147.

172. BARREN HILLS, cat. no. 7.

172

Contributing to O'Shea's decline in popularity after his death was the absence of anyone to organize and show his work. Unlike Armin Hansen, O'Shea had neither an army of students, an artist-wife, nor an immediate family who cared for and promoted his work after his death. Unlike William Ritschel's third wife Elanora ("Nora") Havel, a painter herself, who outlived her husband by many years, Molly O'Shea preceded John in death by sixteen years; she was never as astute and forceful a manager of his artistic output as was Nora of William's—possibly because of their relative prosperity during their life together.

The artist and his work are often forgotten soon after death, only to be revived many years later, if he is fortunate. Fate, however, might be crueler still. In speaking of artists, Edward Hopper (1882–1967) is quoted as having said: "Ninety percent of them are forgotten after they're dead."[376]

Incidentally, Hopper's *Cape Ann Granite*, painted in 1928, and some of his other landscapes, not involving human figures (plate 175), recall strongly a number of works by O'Shea. Judging from the paucity of sales of his paintings—a fact which depressed Hopper considerably—his works were much less appreciated during his lifetime and for some time thereafter than they are today. In 1969 his widow, also a painter, bequeathed some two thousand items to the Whitney Museum in New York.[377]

Indulging in one last reference to a coincidence, however slight, involving Robert Henri and O'Shea, it is recalled that in 1905, while Henri was living at the Sherwood Studios in New York City, he painted one of his female students, Josephine Nivison—"she would one day marry fellow classmate Edward Hopper."[378]

John O'Shea and his paintings were justly famous in their day. It has been a privilege to reassess his life and work and to present them anew—to an audience not having the good fortune to know either the painter or the Carmel of the grand old days.

173

NOTES

Because more than one note was occasionally necessary to document different statements in a sentence, the note numbers of citations appear within the sentence instead of grouped at the end, and encompass the entire text without regard to sections.

Abbreviations for frequently cited sources:

CPC, *Carmel Pine Cone*
E to E, *From Exposition to Exposition: Progressive and Conservative Northern California Painting, 1915–1939*, Joseph A. Baird, Jr., ed.
LAT, *Los Angeles Times*
MPH, *Monterey Peninsula Herald*
SFC, *San Francisco Chronicle*

Detailed citations are given in the bibliography. The O'Shea scrapbook as well as a number of letters, catalogues, photographs, and memorabilia are in the author's possession.

1. The information regarding name changes and the practice of baptizing infants as soon as possible was verified with Professor Sheldon Rothblatt, University of California, Berkeley, as well as with a spokesman for the Consulate General of Ireland in San Francisco.

2. "J. O'Shea Held High Rank in Art," MPH, October 29, 1960; "Collectors' Exchange," *The Gallery* 4 (March 1963), n.p. (This was a publication of The Laky Galleries, Carmel, Calif.)

3. British Passport issued to John O'Shea at San Francisco, California, July 23, 1928.

4. Copy of "Birth and Baptismal Certificate," Diocese of Waterford and Lismore, Parish of Aglish, Ballinameela and Mount Stuart, and letter dated February 22, 1984, at Paroquial House, Aglish, Cappoquin, County Waterford, Ireland, and signed by William Callanan, Parish Priest. Also, letter to author from Father William Callanan, dated July 3, 1984, and copies of Birth and Baptismal Certificates for Maurice Shea and Alice O'Shea.

5. Letters to author from Nora Barry, Ballintaylor, Dungarvan, County Waterford, received August 18 and November 8, 1984. Nora is the wife of John Barry, whose sister Bridget married John O'Shea's brother Maurice.

6. Anna Cora Winchell, "Artists and Their Work," SFC, March 30, 1919, p. E-3.

7. See Virginia McGrath, "John O'Shea," in *Game and Gossip* 5 (May 1952):15, 37. This publication by What's Doing, Inc., Monterey, Calif., was published every six weeks during the year. See Ella Young, *Flowering Dusk*, cited in the bibliography.

8. Handwritten note in ink, located "in one of family Bibles, June 4, 1971," stating various autobiographical facts in the first person.

9. Letter from John J. Devine, Chelsea, London, England, dated November 26, 1984.

10. Nancy D. W. Moure, *Dictionary of Art and Artists in Southern California Before 1930*, p. 184. See also necrology in 1984 ed.

11. Letters from John O'Shea to Mrs. Benjamin H. Pine, Terre Haute, Indiana, dated August 25, 1954, and May 11, 1955. The 1954 letter was addressed to her in Leonia, NJ, while she was visiting her granddaughter, Mrs. George Renner.

12. Courtesy General Research Division, New York Public Library, Fifth Avenue at Forty-second Street, February 27, 1985.

13. For sequence of name changes see p. 139 and n. 374.

14. Correspondence from Adeline Bua to author dated January 30 and February 17, 1984.

15. Biographical sketch of John O'Shea in letter from Mrs. O'Shea to Thomas Carr Howe, Jr., dated April 16 (1934).

16. This statement emanated from Mrs. M. R. Jeppson (Molly), having been made, according to her, by John O'Shea to her grandmother Emma, Mrs. B. H. Pine.

17. Letter from Miss Duane Garrison to author dated June 18, 1984.

18. See, for instance, Dorothy Stevenson, "O'Shea at Crest of His Career," MPH, November 1, 1946.

19. LAT, September 16, 1917, part III, p. 14.

20. Reminiscence of Frances Hussey as told by daughter Molly Jeppson, April 28, 1984. Also see *American Art Annual*, vol. 20, 1923–24.

21. Cited in bibliography.

22. Letter to author from Mariann Touba dated July 17, 1984.

23. Letter to author from William McNaught dated November 9, 1984. This photograph is depicted in William Gerdts, *American Impressionism*, p. 172.

24. Letter to author from R. A. Florio dated July 3, 1984.

25. Undated, unsigned reply received by author from Art Students League, March 5, 1984. The last year of employment, 1942, is in conflict with the year of death, 1940, cited in Patricia P. Havlice, *Index to Artistic Biography*. Havlice's was the only reference volume noted, however, which cites a death date.

26. An unbound pamphlet exists.

27. *Robert Henri, Painter*, p. 115.

28. Much information on John O'Shea, Molly O'Shea, and members of her family came from Mrs. M. R. Jeppson (Molly) during various visits and in correspondence 1983–85.

29. Noël Sullivan, "Molly O'Shea—A Tribute," *The Carmel Cymbal*, October 9, 1941.

30. Letter from Evelyn R. Manning dated December 11, 1984, with enclosed copy of "last entry concerning Mr. Shaughnessy in the 1909 Biographic Register."

31. Letter from Cynthia Cobb Snyder to author dated September 6, 1984, and with copy of entry for John O'Shea in *Thurston's Directory of Pasadena*, 1915–16.

32. LAT, December 7, 1913, part III, p. 7.

33. *Graphic*, December 20, 1913, p. 9.

34. LAT, December 14, 1913, part III, p. 4.

35. "Many Exhibitions During the Week," *The New York Herald*, November 27, 1921. Kingore Galleries' brochure is cited in the bibliography.

36. *The Columbia Encyclopedia*, 1950, p. 1308.

37. *Robert Henri, Painter*, p. 113.

38. This painting was lined in 1984. A facsimile of the inscription was preserved.

39. *Graphic*, February 13, 1915, p. 13.

40. William Innes Homer, *Robert Henri and His Circle*, pp. 173, 199.

41. Ruth Westphal, *Plein Air Painters of California*, p. 180.

42. Lynn Baer Smith, "The Relationship Between Paris, New York and San Francisco," in E to E, p. 13.

43. *Southern California Artists*, p. 176, and illustration of *Haze of Afternoon, Arroyo Seco*, p. 177.

44. See *Maurice Prendergast*, especially *Gloucester*, p. 60; *The Cove*, p. 61 and *Blue Landscape*, p. 162. On p. 14 appear two terms which aptly describe the technique most commonly associated with Prendergast's watercolors: "laying in the water" and "divisionist strokes."

45. See *Southern California Artists*, especially, *Fisherman's Cove, Laguna Beach*, p. 163, and photograph of Heisler Park Beach, p. 13.

178. SCENE IN WEST FIFTY-SEVENTH STREET. Building right of double-decker bus houses The Sherwood Studios, at the corner of Sixth Avenue. In the same block, far right, is the Great Northern Hotel. "Intimate Sketches of New York—No. 360." by Vernon H. Bailey, 1935. Courtesy Museum of the City of New York (see page 40).

46. CPC, August 1, 1918; July 4, 1919; June 10, 1920.

47. Compare LAT, March 1, 1914, part III, p. 4 with May 2, 1915, part III, p. 21, and May 9, 1915, part III, p. 17.

48. *Graphic*, December 19, 1914, p. 13, and December 26, 1914, p. 13 for a two-part article.

49. Letter to author from Barbara Orbach dated February 13, 1984.

50. CPC, May 24, 1917. Presumably the big house which was the residence of the writers Alice McGowan and Grace McGowan Cooke. See Franklin Walker, *Seacoast of Bohemia*, p. 65, cited in the bibliography.

51. Courtesy of Betty Hoag McGlynn Archives and letter dated February 9, 1985.

52. CPC, November 29, 1917.

53. CPC, May 25, 1922.

54. CPC, March 10, 1923.

55. CPC, January 28, 1917.

56. CPC, May 3, 1917.

57. CPC, March 29, 1917.

58. CPC, April 12, 1917.

59. CPC, June 14, 1917.

60. CPC, July 26, 1917.

61. CPC, December 20, 1917.

62. CPC, January 10, 1918.

63. CPC, January 3, 1918, p. 3.

64. We are grateful to Richard Criley of Carmel Highlands for the information he provided on John and Molly O'Shea and their circle in early days.

65. CPC, January 10, 1918.

66. CPC, November 1, 1918; May 22, 1919.

67. CPC, November 20, 1919, p. 3.

68. CPC, June 8, 1922, p. 9.

69. CPC, June 22, 1922.

70. *Paul Dougherty, A Retrospective Exhibition*, p. 9.

71. CPC, November 1, 1917.

72. *Monterey: The Artists View*, p. 14.

73. See Virginia McGrath, "John O'Shea," in *Game and Gossip* 5, pp. 15, 37.

74. Ella Young, p. 300.

75. Newspaper clipping in O'Shea scrapbook, possibly Terre Haute, Indiana, n.d., marked in ink "1922."

76. CPC, June 8, 1922, p. 9.

77. See n. 30.

78. Franklin Walker, p. 13.

79. Letter and enclosures to the author from Bruce A. Reeves dated February 27, 1985.

80. Ruth Westphal, pp. 14, 126.

81. CPC, September 14, 1928.

82. *Paul Dougherty*, p. 17.

83. *Monterey: The Artist's View*, p. 29

84. Reply from National Academy of Design to inquiry, January 4, 1985.

85. CPC, September 23, 1938.

86. Information on the Carmel Art Association was gleaned from the records of the organization with kind permission from Gael Donovan on March 2, 1984.

87. Anna Cora Winchell, "Artists and Their Work," SFC, March 30, 1919, p. E-3.

88. Newspaper clipping untitled, undated, possibly *San Francisco Call*, June 18, 1918, in Archives of California Art file on John O'Shea, The Oakland Museum.

89. See, for instance, CPC, June 8, 1922, p. 3, and February 7, 1925; also known as Finn Von Haakon Frolich, Frölich, or Froelich.

90. Christina Orr-Cahall, *The Art of California*, p. 9.

91. This exhibition notice, cited in the bibliography, is preserved in the O'Shea scrapbook.

92. Mildred Albronda, "Granville Redmond: California Landscape Painter," in *Arts and Antiques* 5, p. 52.

93. CPC, June 26, 1919.

94. CPC, September 25, 1919.

95. CPC, June 8, 1922, p. 9.

96. CPC, June 17, 1920.

97. CPC, July 10, 1919.

98. This brochure, cited in the bibliography, is preserved in the O'Shea scrapbook.

99. CPC, September 15, 1921.

100. CPC, May 29, 1919.

101. The biographical sketch of William Ritschel in *Southern California Artists*, p. 164, summarizes the painter's marriages and many of his travels. It is based to some extent on an unpublished, incomplete biography of William Ritschel by Earl W. Shimmons of New York City, dated March 15, 1954, courtesy Electa Havel Elphand.

102. A sales brochure by the Enos Fauratt Agency, Realtors-Insurance Brokers, Carmel, Calif., n.d., gives the history of the "Castle" as it was built during 1918. Archives of California Art, The Oakland Museum.

103. Margo Burke, "Being 'Famous All Over Town' Amuses Peninsula Author," MPH, September 9, 1984.

104. Cynthia Charters Foley, "Modernism in the Bay Area: The Role of the Art Schools," in E to E, p. 34.

105. Ada Hanifin, "O'Shea Works at Palace," *San Francisco Examiner*, May 6, 1934. This article states that he painted the portrait in Carmel; however, on the reverse of one of the photographic prints of the work O'Shea wrote that he had painted the portrait at the Sherwood Studios in New York in 1922, and that it was photographed by Juley, NY.

106. *New York Tribune*, March 19, 1922. The name Royal Cortissoz does not appear on this clipping in the O'Shea scrapbook. However, this article is attributed to Cortissoz numerous times thereafter, e.g., SFC, April 29, 1934, which states that the critique appeared in *The New York Herald Tribune*.

107. The portrait exhibited (number 9) hangs presently at the top of the staircase leading to the main dining room. Catalogue of exhibition, Archives of California Art, The Oakland Museum.

108. State of New York, Affidavit for License to Marry, Number 13857.

109. Letter from Archimandrite Patrick to "My dear John," n.d., accompanied a copy of the "Russian Manuscript."

110. Passport number 6392 issued at New York, May 31, 1922, no longer exists, but it was referred to in number 3574 issued at San Francisco, Calif., July 23, 1928.

111. Announcement for exhibition: "Arnold Genthe: A Pictorialist and Society," The Oakland Museum, February 1985.

112. Franklin Walker, p. 24.

113. See, for instance, Ada King Wallis, "Eminent in the World of Art," in *The Western Woman* 13, p. 64.

114. Letter from John J. Devine, Chelsea, London, England, dated February 2, 1985.

115. CPC, March 17, 1923, p. 7.

116. There exists a stamped and canceled envelope addressed by Mrs. B. H. Pine to a Mrs. Frank A. Brogan, 3811 Deney Avenue, Omaha, Nebraska (October 11, 1957), which was returned undelivered. On it appears in purple ink the inscription "large painting of Grandma," which like the name and Omaha, Nebraska, is circled in purple ink. One surmises that a relationship between this name and *Grandma* was known to Mrs. Pine.

117. CPC, June 2, 1923, p. 7.

118. Helen Bruton, Monterey, Calif., remembers having beach parties here "many years ago." Personal communication October 1984.

119. CPC, October 27, 1923, p. 8.

120. CPC, April 26, 1924.

121. CPC, November 29, 1924.

122. CPC, November 29, 1924, p. 8.

123. "Carmel Artist's South Sea Work Exhibited Here," SFC, May 1, 1934.

BIRCHES, detail of plate 113.

124. Letterhead (see n. 15) reads Tynalacan, Box 166, Rural Route, Carmel, California.

125. CPC, March 28, 1937.

126. Ella Young offered a vivid description of this picnic area in *Flowering Dusk*, p. 300. See also CPC, Nov. 20, 1931, p. 7; clearly the O'Sheas owned more property than is indicated in present assessor records (see n. 79).

127. Realtor Rose Ulman of Carmel Highlands provided much information from memory on John O'Shea and on her husband's real-estate transactions with him.

128. CPC, August 19, 1932, p. 28.

129. Ella Young, pp. 188–90.

130. CPC, February 1, 1935.

131. Letter from John O'Shea to Emma Pine dated May 11, 1955.

132. Edward L. Korb, *A Biographical Index to California and Western Artists*, p. 152.

133. CPC, November 24, 1923.

134. There is some confusion about the time of William Ritschel's trips to the South Seas and the length of stay on each trip. In *Southern California Artists*, p. 164 one reads that Ritschel's first voyage to the South Seas was in 1922; however, a typewritten manuscript by Ritschel referred to here and cited in the bibliography is dated July 23, 1923. A copy of this was owned by O'Shea. See n. 135.

135. CPC, October 27, 1923, p. 1. This news item states that Ritschel has just returned from a sixteen-month sojourn. Possibly the journey included part of 1922 and 1923.

136. CPC, May 12, 1921. Probably meant was Lucien J. Simon (1861–1945).

137. CPC, November 17, 1917, and September 14, 1928, p. 2.

138. CPC, October 10, 1930, pp. 1–2.

139. CPC, March 23, 1923, p. 1.

140. See especially Franklin Walker, p. 105; also CPC, June 30, 1921, for cast of characters.

141. Letter from "Pop" Hart to John O'Shea dated July 8, 1923.

142. CPC, September 20, 1924, p. 1.

143. CPC, January 17, 1925.

144. Franklin Walker, pp. 119–20.

145. CPC, October 24, 1930.

146. CPC, June 7, 1917; October 21, 1920; April 19 and 26, 1929.

147. CPC, October 27, 1923, p. 1; January 17, 1925; December 10, 1925.

148. CPC, May 22, 1926, p. 14. Although this article refers to Elanora, Electa Havel Elphand, Mill Valley, Calif., stated that her sister was never given the name Elanora, but may have used it for a short time in New York City, "where she may have experimented with it" (March 6, 1985). Nevertheless, the author noticed that the marriage certificate of "Nora" to William Ritschel in Reno, Nevada, bore the name Elanora (March 10, 1985).

149. CPC, October 24, 1930.

150. CPC, April 3, 1931, p. 16.

151. CPC, June 5, 1931, p. 4.

152. CPC, September 19, 1925. Again in spring of 1929, she spent several months in the East while Shawn remained at the Highlands. CPC, May 31, 1929, p. 14.

153. CPC, June 11, 1926, p. 11.

154. There exists a painting of a mountain village which was orginally thought to be Nogales, Mexico, but is clearly Valdez, New Mexico. Compare with woodcut of *Valdez, New Mexico* by Esther Bruton (Gilman), *The Carmelite*, December 26, 1928, p. 1.

155. Ella Young, "Charcoals of John O'Shea," CPC, May 25, 1934; especially description of "barn-yard chick."

156. SFC, May 1, 1934.

157. CPC, June 18, 1926, p. 11.

158. CPC, August 6, 1926, p. 11; August 13, 1926, p. 11.

159. CPC, October 15, 1926.

160. See William Innes Homer, p. 264. Mary Fanton Roberts, a writer, was one of the first supporters of "The Eight" (see p. 139 in n. 161).

161. *Robert Henri, Painter*, p. 83.

162. William Innes Homer, pp. 286–87.

163. CPC featured many entries on this subject during August–September, 1927.

164. CPC, October 14, 1927, p. 5; October 21, 1927, p. 1.

165. SFC, December 11, 1927, p. D-7; CPC, December 30, 1927, p. 4.

166. CPC, January 20, 1928, p. 5.

167. CPC, January 27, 1928, p. 4.

168. CPC, July 9, 1926, p. 3.

169. CPC, July 29, 1926, p. 6.

170. Terry St. John, *Society of Six*, p. 13.

171. CPC, January 20, 1928, p. 5.

172. CPC, January 27, 1928, p. 5.

173. Noted courtesy Joseph A. Baird, Jr.

174. Lynn Baer Smith, "The Relationship Between Paris, New York and San Francisco," in E to E, p. 18.

175. Aline Kistler, "'Change' in O'Shea's Work Discussed," SFC, May 13, 1928, p. 43; and CPC, May 18, 1928, p. 4.

176. Jehanne Biétry Salinger, "Desert Paintings," *San Francisco Examiner*, May 13, 1928.

177. CPC, December 23, 1922; August 10, 1928, p. 2.

178. CPC, August 17, 1928. For other farewell and welcome-home parties in connection with this voyage, see *The Carmelite*, August 1, p. 3; August 8, p. 3; October 24, p. 8; November 7, 1928, p. 5.

179. "O'Sheas Sail For Tahiti," newspaper clipping, n.d., no source, in O'Shea scrapbook with illustration of Molly and John. An item on the reverse carries the date of August 9.

180. Issued at San Francisco, July 23, 1928, number 3574.

181. Ella Young, pp. 297, 301.

182. Three small documents relating to their voyage to Tahiti are in the O'Shea scrapbook.

183. CPC, November 16, 1928, p. 14.

184. Molly O'Shea's Certificate of Naturalization is number 2865758; John's Certificate of Citizenship is number 3198285, dated February 3, 1930.

185. CPC, August 12, 1927, p. 7. See also several weeks following for rapidly developing Association plans.

186. CPC, February 7, 1928, p. 4.

187. See n. 86; CPC, June 21, p. 9; July 5, p. 6; July 12, 1929.

188. We have not determined where "ORDING" studio or photographer was located.

189. Nancy Newhall, *The Daybooks of Edward Weston, Volume II. California*, p. 142.

190. Ibid., p. 119.

191. Ibid., p. 142.

192. Ibid., pp. 187, 211.

193. CPC, December 8, 1921, gives the announcement of the marriage of Vasia Anikeyef to Sybil Brainard.

194. Both D. Kirke Erskine and Rose Ulman, Carmel, indicated that the statue was an image of the Irish poet and remembered when it adorned the O'Sheas' "Cliff Property."

195. CPC, October 9, 1931, p. 8; December 25, 1931, p. 7.

196. Ella Winter, "Poet and Painter Meet on the South Seas," *The Carmelite*, April 3, 1929, p. 3.

197. CPC, May 11, 1928, p. 4.

198. Nancy Newhall, pp. 187, 211–12.

199. Ibid., p. 212.

200. Ibid., pp. 237–38, for example.

201. Ibid., p. 147; illustrated as plate 10.

202. Some of these prints are now in the collection of Mr. and Mrs. M. R. Jeppson, Carmel.

203. Edward Weston, "O'Shea," Art Notes, *The Carmelite*, April 2, 1931.

204. Nancy Newhall, p. 174.

205. Ibid., p. 169.

206. Franklin Walker, p. 66.

207. CPC, July 15, 1927, p. 11.

208. *The Carmelite*, April 2, 1930, announces the visit in Monterey of Sinclair Lewis and his wife, Dorothy Thompson, and their imminent departure for Los Angeles.

209. Ella Young, pp. 300–01.

210. Nancy Newhall, pp. 143, 149. Weston met Ella Young, Tony and Mabel Dodge Luhan, February 25, 1930.

211. Letter to Dear O'Shea from G. A. Scott, 1342½ Laurel Avenue, Hollywood, California, dated January 16, 1930.

212. There is some confusion in the titles of certain paintings, we believe, due to the similarity of three Spanish words. *Morada* is the name of a meeting house or chapel of the Penitentes, mistakenly spelled *Marada*. *Mirada*, a view or lookout point, was the title of a painting O'Shea showed at the California Palace of the Legion of Honor in 1934, most probably known today as *Grand Canyon No. 1*. A work titled MARADA (surely a MORADA) appears on the cover of *The Gallery* (a publication of the Laky Galleries, Carmel) dated March 1965, and is listed for sale as number 20. This work's location today is unknown.

213. For brief accounts of Mabel Dodge Luhan's stay in Taos, New Mexico, see Mary Carroll Nelson, *The Legendary Artists of Taos*.

214. Ibid., p. 164.

215. *The Carmelite*, May 15, 1930, p. 11.

216. Mary Carroll Nelson, p. 170. There is confusion regarding the year of Henri's second visit to Santa Fe. Here we read 1918, while in William Innes Homer, p. 202, it is 1917.

217. Doris Ostrander Dawdy, *Artists of the American West*, vol. 1, p. 86.

218. CPC, October 10, 1930, pp. 1–2.

219. Ella Young, p. 30.

220. CPC, November 28, 1930, p. 14.

221. Newspaper clipping, p. 5, bears title: "On the Beach at Waikiki; Beach Boy • Sun Tan • Malihini" superimposed over an image of Diamond Head mountain. O'Shea scrapbook.

222. O'Shea scrapbook.

223. This work was purchased in 1937 from O'Shea by William Henry Black of Sonoma, California. He was a friend of John, Martin Flavin, and Hilaire Belloc. (Letter dated April 3, 1984.)

224. "John O'Shea's Exhibit," *The Carmelite*, March 26, 1931.

225. CPC, March 20, 1931, p. 4.

226. CPC, December 11, 1931, p. 8, and December 18, 1931, p. 20; Marjorie Tait, "Studio Gossip," CPC, June 10, 1932, p. 7.

227. CPC, June 24, 1932, p. 8.

228. CPC, August 19, 1932, p. 17.

229. CPC, September 16, 1932, p. 5.

230. CPC, December 9, 1932, p. 1.

231. *The Carmelite*, September 8, 1932, p. 4.

232. Edward Weston, "The John O'Shea Exhibition," CPC, March 10, 1933.

233. MPH, February 14, 1933.

234. MPH, March 9, 1933.

235. "Carmel Man Paints Soul of Steffens, Muckraker," *Oakland Tribune*, February 9, 1933. See also CPC, February 17, 1933, p. 11.

236. "Highlands Artist Has Stanford Exhibition," CPC, November 17, 1933, p. 5.

237. Josephine Mildred Blanch, "Tropical, Desert Themes Feature O'Shea Exhibit," MPH, September 14, 1933. See also CPC, August 25, 1933, p. 33.

238. John Douglas Short, "John O'Shea," *Controversy*, November 2, 1934, p. 9.

239. Obituary, "John O'Shea," *The Carmel Pine Cone-Cymbal*, May 3, 1956.

240. Letters and postcards preserved with O'Shea scrapbook.

241. "Carmel Artist Exhibits Work Before Art Club; John O'Shea Shows Paintings for First Time in Sacramento," undated (but surely March 1935), no source, preserved in O'Shea scrapbook.

242. As noted in an article in CPC, September 30, 1932, Carmel Valley growers produced large quantities of pears which "were ready to be shipped out." O'Shea painted a number of orchard scenes.

243. MPH, September 14, 1933.

244. Pauline J. Rollins, "International Art Deco in Northern California, 1915–1919," in E to E, p. 57.

245. CPC, February 23, 1934, p. 5.

246. CPC, March 23, 1934, p. 5; August 24, 1934, p. 27.

247. Letter from Thomas Carr Howe, Jr., to John O'Shea, August 14, 1933.

248. CPC, February 1, 1935.

249. Jackson M. Dodge, "Patrons and Collectors: (part B). Albert Bender and the Early Years of the San Francisco Museum of Art," in E to E, p. 41. James D. Hart states that Bender arrived in San Francisco in 1883.

250. J. D. S. (John Douglas Short), "Art Notes," *Controversy*, November 2, 1934, p. 9.

251. James D. Hart, *A Companion to California*, p. 36.

252. List of sixty-three "Paintings and Drawings" exhibited at the California Palace of the Legion of Honor, in O'Shea scrapbook; also copy of same obtained from the museum, January 24, 1985.

253. Copies of all correspondence relating to the John O'Shea exhibition were received through the courtesy of Debra L. Pughe, Exhibitions Manager, on January 24, 1985. There exists a set of photographs of paintings produced by Lewis Josselyn of Carmel which were almost certainly ordered in connection with the exhibition. Although fewer in number than those exhibited, they match many of the titles on the list of works exhibited. See n. 252.

254. Ella Young, p. 222.

255. Letter from Noël Sullivan to Lloyd L. Rollins dated April 1, 1933.

256. Reply from L. L. Rollins to Noël Sullivan dated April 3, 1933.

257. All of these documents preserved in the O'Shea scrapbook.

258. *Oakland Tribune*, April 29, 1934.

259. SFC, May 1, 1934.

260. *Mill Valley Record*, May 4, 1934.

261. Junius Cravens, "O'Shea, After Six Years Among South Sea Natives, Desert Indians, Exhibits at Palace," *San Francisco News*, April 28, 1934.

262. "No Bread," *The Argonaut*, San Francisco, May 18, 1934.

263. See list, n. 252.

264. Nancy Newhall, p. 142.

265. CPC, May 25, 1934.

266. MPH, November 3, 1956, p. A 2.

267. Ella Young, pp. 301–03.

268. MPH, October 31, 1947; November 3, 1952, p. A 9.

269. Letters from John O'Shea to Emma Pine dated August 25 and September 1, no year, but probably 1954.

270. "Waterford Artist in U.S." On the reverse of this undated newspaper clipping, no source, one reads of "pounds," "*Independent* readers" and "recognised" with an "s," indicating most likely that it is *The Irish Independent*, Dublin. A photograph of John O'Shea is included; the original, known today, is signed Arnold Genthe, New York. These items are in the O'Shea scrapbook.

271. Letter to author from Curator Ethna Waldron dated June 11, 1984.

272. *The Columbia Encyclopedia*, 1950, p. 974.

273. A copy of Ferdinand Perret's artists' file, on index cards, is maintained in the Archives of California Art, The Oakland Museum.

274. See p. 43 in n. 249.

275. Christine Giles, "Patrons and Collectors: (part A). Early Influences on Collecting of Modern Art in California," in E to E, p. 39.

276. CPC, September 21, 1934, p. 1.

277. CPC, October 5, 1934, p. 9; October 12, 1934, p. 16.

278. CPC, October 19, 1934, p. 4.

279. CPC, November 23, 1934, p. 6.

280. Thelma B. Miller, CPC, January 11, 1935, p. 3.

281. CPC, February 8, 1935, p. 8.

282. CPC, March 8, 1935, p. 9.

283. Sadly none of the four reviews of the Sacramento exhibition indicates the source; one is dated March 2, 1935. Another, clearly a Sacramento paper, gives the interesting comment presented here. The clipping is in the O'Shea scrapbook.

284. *Crocker Art Museum Handbook of Paintings*, p. 69.

285. CPC, March 1, 1935, p. 2; a Sacramento paper (see n. 283), March 2, 1935.

286. CPC, August 16, 1935, p. 7.

287. CPC, June 7, 1935, p. 10.

288. Twenty-eight works are listed (three added in handwriting) in pamphlet "Exhibition of Paintings by John O'Shea, Subjects of Mexico."

289. This and an additional preliminary list on wrapping paper are preserved in the O'Shea scrapbook.

290. CPC, August 16, 1935, p. 7, indicates that the O'Sheas were "in Mexico City for the past five months" and that he had "been sketching and painting." According to Mrs. Dan James (March 5, 1985), the "D. L." Jameses and the O'Sheas either went to Mexico together on *several occasions* or met there in the 1930s.

VALDEZ, *ca.* 1930, detail of plate 78.

291. Irene Alexander, "Top Flight Art Show in Carmel," probably MPH, week of June 18, 1945. Undated clipping, no source, preserved in O'Shea scrapbook.

292. MPH, July 13, 1962. Apparently, Dickinson was a good friend of O'Shea. See Nancy Newhall, p. 187.

293. Thelma B. Miller, "Paintings of Mexican People Made Human by Brush of John O'Shea," CPC, September 27, 1935, p. 10. A curious title with which John O'Shea himself was in all likelihood not satisfied [auth.].

294. "O'Shea Canvas Adorns Library," CPC, April 16, 1937.

295. Virginia McGrath, "Burton Shepard Boundey," in *Game and Gossip* 5, pp. 5, 35.

296. Undated brief note received by author from the Art Institute of Chicago on April 2, 1984.

297. See, for instance, Mahonri Sharp Young, *The Eight*, pp. 20–21; *Robert Henri, Painter*, p. 99.

298. Mahonri Sharp Young, p. 38.

299. William Innes Homer, pp. 111–12.

300. Mahonri Sharp Young, p. 23.

301. *Robert Henri, Painter*, p. 71.

302. Ibid., pp. 123–25.

303. Ibid., p. 123.

304. Ibid., p. 125.

305. William Innes Homer, p. 255. The author received on February 23, 1985, from Janet J. LeClair, Robert Henri's heir, a copy of the artist's sketch of "Chinese Girl" also known as "Chow Choy"; her occidental name, "Mary," appears in small handwriting on the sketching paper, as well as the fact that it had been shown at Los Angeles in 1914.

306. CPC, September 27, 1935.

307. *Robert Henri, Painter*, p. 141. (See n. 216 for uncertainty of year of Henri's second visit to Santa Fe.)

308. Ibid., p. 161.

309. *Landscape Upstate*, ca. 1930, a watercolor by George Luks and *Centaurs and Nymphs*, 1921, a watercolor by George "Pop" Overbury Hart were both seen by the author in the exhibition: *Works on Paper*, on loan from the Hirshhorn Museum and Sculpture Garden, at the Monterey Peninsula Museum of Art, July 29, 1984. Excerpts from the inaugural exhibition catalogue of the Hirshhorn appear in *American Art Review* 2 (March–April 1975), and *Centaurs and Nymphs* is depicted on p. 91.

310. See letter of George Hart to John O'Shea dated May 10, 1924, preserved with O'Shea scrapbook.

311. *The Prints of George Overbury ("Pop") Hart*, Bethesda Art Gallery. This pamphlet contains a short essay and some illustrations of Hart's work.

312. The details of this exhibition have not been located.

313. Wesley M. Burnside, *Maynard Dixon*, p. 129, relates the work of Dixon to "a modified form of this [cubism] called cubist realism" as discussed at length by Milton W. Brown, *American Painting from the Armory Show to the Depression*.

314. CPC, November 27, 1919.

315. CPC, November 18, 1920. See, however, CPC, June 30, 1933, p. 13, for a departure from "his newer manner."

316. See Wesley M. Burnside, p. 130.

317. *Robert Henri, Painter*, p. 73. These valuable notebooks are preserved today by Henri's heir Janet J. LeClair.

318. A letter from Olga Epstein Interiors signed by Miss Epstein of San Francisco to Mr. and Mrs. O'Shea, dated October 22, 1936, tells of her fascination with O'Shea's *Bananas* and of her cousin Alice Klauber's plan to acquire the work for the Gallery. She was at that time the Chairman of the Purchasing Committee of the Fine Arts Society. The transaction, however, apparently never took place.

319. CPC, February 5, 1937.

320. *News Flashes*, May 1, 1937, gives brief biographies of the artists featured that month in addition to John O'Shea: Umberto Romano, John Young-Hunter, and Kenneth Adams.

321. Letter from Otto Wittmann, Jr., Registrar, Nelson Gallery, for "Friends of Art," Kansas City, Missouri, dated June 25, 1937.

322. Nancy Newhall, pp. 133–34.

323. CPC, June 18, 1937.

324. CPC, October 29, 1937.

325. Margaret Hensel, "Martin Flavin," in *Game and Gossip* 5, pp. 2, 32.

326. CPC, August 11, 1921; May 25, 1922.

327. *The Carmelite*, April 24, 1930.

328. Mr. and Mrs. Sean (Rebecca) Flavin, Monterey, Calif., offered interesting information regarding his father's friendship with John O'Shea; February–March 1984.

329. CPC, December 10, 1937; January 7, 1938.

330. CPC, May 20, 1938, p. 6.

331. Elaborating somewhat, Howard's use of watercolor in his fine and very detailed work requires an absorbent surface because many "layers" of color are often applied and need to "sink in" (March 4, 1985).

332. CPC, August 12, 1938; August 26, 1938, p. 14.

333. Micaela Martinez DuCasse of Piedmont, Calif., recalls (January 1, 1985) meeting John O'Shea and seeing this house when the O'Sheas lived in it and later when it was the home of Emily Colby. Micaela's mother, Elsie Whitaker Martinez, and her friend Harriett Dean were on "lookout duty" in a small house near "Tynalacan" in the 1940s after the Pearl Harbor attack.

334. CPC, March 28, 1937.

335. Patricia Sheldahl French, "California Painting at the Golden Gate International Exposition," in E to E, p. 61.

336. Robert D. Kinsman (Swope Gallery Director), "Art from Swope," unknown publication, dated in handwriting "March 1982." The article features an illustration of *Monterey Cypress* and states that its date is 1939. However, a photograph exists of the work which is believed to have been taken for the purpose of publicity in connection with the 1934 exhibition at the California Palace of the Legion of Honor. See page 116 and n. 253.

337. See numerous references to Eugen Neuhaus in E to E.

338. MPH, September 24, 1940.

339. CPC, July 7, 1923, p. 12.

340. See *Del Monte Revisited* for articles on this renowned gallery and the quotation from the article by Josephine Mildred Blanch, which follows here, reprinted from *Art in Progress* 5, no. 11, (1914).

341. This quotation courtesy of Betty Hoag McGlynn Archives, Carmel, Calif. Inexplicably, records of The Dayton Art Institute searched to date have not revealed a mention of this event. Letter to author from Helen L. Pinkney, dated February 22, 1985.

342. Noël Sullivan, "Molly O'Shea—A Tribute," *The Carmel Cymbal*, October 9, 1941.

343. See n. 10 as well as Nancy Moure, *Painting and Sculpture in Los Angeles*.

Paintings of Arizona and California by John O'Shea, exhibition catalogue. Pasadena, Calif.: The Grace Nicholson Galleries, 1928.

The Prints of George Overbury ("Pop") Hart, exhibition catalogue. Bethesda, Maryland: Bethesda Art Gallery, 1984.

Robert Henri, Painter, exhibition catalogue. Wilmington, Del.: Delaware Art Museum, 1984.

Santiago, Danny. *Famous All Over Town*. New York: Simon and Schuster, 1983.

St. John, Terry. *Society of Six*, exhibition catalogue. Oakland, Calif.: The Oakland Museum, 1972.

Southern California Artists, 1890–1940, exhibition catalogue. Laguna Beach, Calif.: Laguna Beach Museum of Art, 1979.

Spangenberg, Helen. *Yesterday's Artists on the Monterey Peninsula*. Monterey, Calif.: Monterey Peninsula Museum of Art, 1976.

Walker, Franklin. *The Seacoast of Bohemia*. Santa Barbara, Calif. and Salt Lake City, Utah: Peregrine Smith, Inc., 1973.

Wallis, Ada King. "Eminent in the World of Art." *The Western Woman* 13 (nos. 2–3, n.d.): 64–65. (No articles mention date later than 1949; N. Moure gives date 1951 for "revised edition.")

Westphal, Ruth Lilly. *Plein Air Painters of California. The Southland*. Irvine, Calif.: Westphal Publishing, 1982.

Whitton, Donald C., and Johnson, Robert E. *Percy Gray, 1869–1952*, exhibition catalogue. San Francisco: California Historical Society, 1970.

Young, Ella. *Flowering Dusk, Things Remembered Accurately and Inaccurately*. New York: Longmans, Green and Co., 1945.

Young, Mahonri Sharp. *The Eight: The Realist Revolt in American Painting*. New York: Watson-Guptill Publications, 1973.

179. George Overbury "Pop" Hart, SPRINGTIME IN NEW ORLEANS. Lithograph, 9½″ × 12⅝″, dedicated to John O'Shea by the artist (see page 132).

Catalogue of Works by John O'Shea

I. KNOWN WORKS

In this section, we list alphabetically by present title all known and located works by John O'Shea. Cited for each work are dimensions in inches (height before width), medium, support, and location of signature—either that of the artist or the estate stamp. Where known the date is stated. Date approximations are based on the earliest known exhibition record or mention of the work, which is also indicated. Where known, previous titles are given in parentheses. Present owners listed are cited with their kind permission or remain anonymous by request. Where ownership is omitted, the works are in the collection of WIM Fine Arts, Oakland, California.

Approximately seventeen additional known works—mostly large oil paintings—recorded in the mid-1960s, were either not made available now for cataloguing or could not be located.

Abbreviations used:

C, center
CAA, Carmel Art Association
CPC, *Carmel Pine Cone*
CPLH, California Palace of the Legion of Honor, San Francisco, 1934
D-WG, Denny-Watrous Gallery, Carmel
Exh., exhibited
FMC, Friday Morning Club, Los Angeles, 1915
GNG, Grace Nicholson Galleries, Pasadena, 1928
HDMG, Hotel Del Monte Gallery, Monterey
HGP, Hotel Green, Pasadena, 1914
HGSF, Helgesen Gallery, San Francisco, 1919
HWWL, a handwritten list on white stationery
Illus., illustrated
KG, Kingore Galleries, New York, 1921
L, lower, in first place; left, in second
LAMA, Los Angeles Museum of Art
LAT, *Los Angeles Times*
LGC, Laky Galleries, Carmel
Lloyds, a fine arts insurance policy was issued to John O'Shea by United States Lloyds, Inc., New York, dated May 31, 1924, for six paintings
MEC, John O'Shea Memorial Exhibition, CAA, October 1956
MPH, *Monterey Peninsula Herald*
n(s)., reference footnote(s) in text
No(s)., number(s) at exhibitions or in this catalogue
P2L, a list of names on "p.2" of a letter, no date, in O'Shea scrapbook
R, right
SAG, Stanford Art Gallery, Fall 1933
SFAA, San Francisco Art Association
U, upper
22L, a list with twenty-two items, no date, in O'Shea scrapbook
1931E, a list on an envelope dated March 21, 1931, in O'Shea scrapbook

OIL PAINTINGS

1. ALMOND TREES IN BLOOM
   (ORCHARD or PEAR TREES)
   Oil on canvas
   32 × 28
   Not signed
   Emma-Rose Layton
   Illus. as ORCHARD in *The Gallery* 2, no. 5 (Christmas 1964), and as PEAR TREES on LGC brochure, July–August 1967

2. ANGRY SEA
   Oil on canvas
   44 × 54
   Estate signed LR

3. ARIZONA DESERT
   Oil on canvas
   25 × 30
   Estate signed LL

4. AUTUMN REFLECTIONS
   Artist's title
   Oil on canvas
   25 × 30
   Estate signed LR

5. BANANA BLOSSOMS, *ca.* 1928
   Oil on canvas
   36 × 30½
   Signed LR
   Five paintings entitled *Tahitian Bananas* were listed for exhibition in the 1934 show at CPLH (Nos. 5–9). We have photographs of four of these taken at that time (Lewis Josselyn, Carmel). Today we know and record four banana works, each bearing a different title. Of these, one is the same as originally photographed, one (*Tahitian Bananas 2*) shows slight modification, and two were not among those previously photographed. Therefore, at least six works were painted of which two are unknown. See n. 253

6. BANANA FOLIAGE, *ca.* 1928
   Oil on canvas
   36 × 30
   Signed LR

7. BARREN HILLS
   (BARE HILLS)
   Oil on canvas
   25 × 30
   Estate signed LR
   Exh. Carmel Valley Art Gallery, n.d.

8. BIG SUR COAST
   (COAST FOG)
   Oil on canvas
   22 × 27½
   Signed LR
   Mrs. W. M. Hussey
   Illus. MPH, Oct. 31, 1947

9. BIRCHES
   Oil on canvas
   24 × 30
   Estate signed LR
   Perhaps these are liquid amber or canoe birch. A description of THE SILVER SCREEN in 1915, n. 47, fits this work. Exh. LGC, 1965

10. BIRD OF PARADISE, *ca.* 1931
    Oil on composition board
    48 × 36
    Estate signed LC
    Exh. D-WG, 1931
    Illus. *Carmel Valley Outlook*, Mar. 17, 1975

11. BLIND WOMAN OF TAOS, *ca.* 1930
    (OLD MIDWIFE-TAOS or OLD MEXICAN WOMAN)
    Oil on canvas
    36 × 30
    Estate signed UL
    Exh. D-WG, 1931
    In early photograph, a painting, now overpainted, was placed in upper left corner.

12. BLUE PACIFIC
    Oil on canvas
    20 × 24
    Estate signed LR
    Owner anonymous

13. BLUE POOL
    Oil on board
    22 × 28
    Estate signed LL

14. BLUE SEA, *ca.* 1919
    Artist's title
    Oil on board
    16 × 20
    Signed LR
    Owner anonymous
    Exh. HGSF, No. 20

15. BOY (Indian or Mexican)
    Oil on canvas board
    13¼ × 10¾
    Signed UR
    Mrs. W. M. Hussey

16. CALIFORNIA HILLS
    Oil on canvas
    25 × 30
    Estate signed LL

17. CARNIVAL
    (DESIGN or CHINESE PATTERN)
    Oil on board
    11½ × 14½
    Signed LL

18. CHINA COVE
    Oil on canvas
    21¾ × 27½
    Not signed
    Pamela O'Meara

19. CHINA COVE BEACH
    (CARMEL COAST)
    Oil on masonite
    20 × 24
    Authenticated by Emma Pine
    Gary Breitweiser

20. COAST HILLS
    Oil on canvas
    34 × 40
    Estate signed LR

21. COAST HILLS, CARMEL VALLEY
    Oil on composition board
    20 × 24
    Signed LL
    LGC label

22. COAST PINES-HIGHLANDS
    Oil on canvas
    30 × 36
    Estate signed LR

23. COASTAL SCENE
    Oil on canvas board
    16 × 20
    Not signed
    Molly Knox

24. COASTLANDS
    Oil on board
    11½ × 13¾
    Estate signed LR
    Owner anonymous

25. COLORED MOUNTAINS, *ca.* 1927
    (CANELO HILLS; portion of label on reverse)
    Oil on canvas
    30 × 36
    Signed LL
    Exh. GNG, No. 13.
    Probably exh. at CPLH as MAGIC MOUNTAINS, ARIZONA, which name was interchangeable with SUPERSTITION MOUNTAINS. See Nos. 67, 557 here

26. COLORFUL HIGHLANDS
    Oil on canvas
    34 × 40
    Estate signed LR

27. COMIDA, MARKET DAY, *ca.* 1936
    Oil on canvas
    54 × 64
    Signed LR
    Harrison Memorial Library, Carmel

28. CORSAIR, *ca.* 1921
    Oil on canvas
    30 × 36
    Signed LR

29. COSMOS
    Oil on canvas
    30 × 25
    Signed LR
    William and Grace Davis

30. COVE AT SUNSET
    Oil on canvas
    28 × 36
    Signed LR
    Inscription on reverse: A. Lenique, 1911

31. CYPRESS POINT
    Oil on canvas
    25 × 30
    Authenticated by Emma Pine
    Mr. and Mrs. James F. Morris

32. CYPRESS TREES
    Oil on canvas
    30 × 36
    Estate signed LL

33. DAHLIAS, *ca.* 1920
    (VASE OF FLOWERS)
    Oil on canvas
    33 × 29
    Signed LC
    Molly Jeppson
    Exh. CPLH, No. 16. See CPC, Sept. 10, 1937

34. DARK ROCKS
   Oil on canvas
   25 × 30
   Estate signed LR
   Owner anonymous

35. DIADEM-TAHITI,
   ca. 1928
   Oil on canvas
   25 × 30
   Not signed
   Mrs. W. M. Hussey

36. DOWN NEAR
   NEPENTHE (pre-1935)
   (COAST AND PINES)
   25 × 30
   Signed LR
   Cynthia Criley Williams

37. DOWN THE COAST
   (MARINE)
   Oil on canvas
   34 × 40
   Signed LL
   Illus. MPH, Oct. 29, 1948

38. EARLY BLOSSOMS
   (ALMOND TREES)
   Oil on canvas
   25 × 30
   Authenticated by
   Emma Pine
   Gary Breitweiser

39. EARLY SPRING,
   ARIZONA
   (TANQUE VERDE HILLS;
   portion of label on reverse)
   Oil on canvas
   25 × 30
   Signed LR
   Exh. GNG, No. 11

40. ELEPHANT EARS
   36 × 30
   Oil on canvas
   Not signed
   Molly Jeppson

41. EUCALYPTUS TREES IN
   STORM, *ca.* 1915
   (REVELRY)
   Oil on canvas
   36 × 28
   Signed LR
   Mrs. W. M. Hussey
   Illus. in *Graphic*, Feb. 13,
   1915

42. FAR MOUNTAINS
   Artist's title
   Oil on canvas
   25 × 30
   Estate signed LR

43. FLAME TREES
   Oil on canvas
   25 × 30
   Signature not visible
   Anne Dickman-Grant

44. FLOWERING HILLS,
   ca. 1933
   (OAHU HILLS, probably
   early title)
   Oil on canvas
   25 × 30
   Signed LL
   Exh. SAG; HDMG, 1933

45. FLOWERING ORCHARD
   Oil on canvas
   25 × 30
   Estate signed LR

46. FRUIT TREES
   Oil on canvas
   25 × 30
   Signed LR

47. FURIOUS SURF
   Oil on canvas
   34 × 40
   Estate signed LR
   LGC label

48. GOLDEN HILLS
   Oil on composition board
   20 × 24
   Estate signed LL

49. GRAND CANYON NO. 1,
   ca. 1930
   (MIRADA was probable
   title in early exh.)
   Oil on canvas
   30 × 36
   Signed LR
   Exh. CPLH, No. 24

50. GRAND CANYON NO. 2
   Oil on canvas
   25 × 30
   Estate signed LR

51. GRANDMA, *ca.* 1921
   Oil on canvas
   46 × 44
   Signed LR
   Exh. KG, No. 6. See p. 36
   for discussion of this work

52. GRASS AND HILLS
   Oil on canvas
   34 × 40
   Estate signed LL

53. GRASSY HILLS
   Oil on canvas
   30 × 40
   Estate signed LR

54. HAWAIIAN LANDSCAPE,
   ca. 1928
   Oil on canvas
   25 × 30
   Not signed
   Jane Johnson
   Perhaps Tahiti

55. HIDEAWAY, *ca.* 1921
   Oil on canvas
   25 × 30
   Estate signed LR

56. HOLY MAN, *ca.* 1935
   Oil on academy board
   20 × 18
   Signed LR
   One of a series of 3 painted
   of a "Holy Man" in Mexico.
   See No. 114 here and CPC,
   Dec. 10, 1937

57. INDIAN
   Oil on canvas
   30 × 25
   Signed LL
   Jane Renner

58. INDIANA AUTUMN
   Oil (presumably on canvas)
   30 × 35
   Authenticated by
   Emma Pine
   Mrs. George H. Macy

59. INSIDE THE REEF,
   ca. 1931
   (KEWALO BASIN,
   HAWAII, or WITHIN THE
   REEFS)
   Oil on canvas
   25 × 30
   Signed LL
   Exh. D-WG, 1931

60. JUNGLE STREAM,
   ca. 1928
   Oil on canvas board
   20 × 16
   Estate signed LL
   Probably a Tahitian banana
   grove

61. LATE AUTUMN
   (CARMEL VALLEY)
   Oil on canvas
   29 × 36
   Signed LL
   Anne Dickman-Grant
   Illus. MPH, Oct. 29, 1960

62. LEI WOMAN
   Oil on canvas
   36 × 40
   No visible signature
   Anne Dickman-Grant
   Exh. D-WG, 1931; CPLH;
   E. B. Crocker Art Gallery,
   Sacramento, 1935; MEC

63. LOW TIDE, MOUTH
   CARMEL RIVER
   Oil on canvas
   16 × 20
   Estate signed LL

64. LUPIN AND POPPIES
   Oil on canvas
   24 × 30
   Signed LL
   Dr. and Mrs. Sydney T.
   Wright

65. LUSH FOLIAGE, *ca.* 1928
   Oil on canvas
   25 × 30
   Signed LL
   Probably Tahitian banana
   grove

66. MADRONE, *ca.* 1921
   (LANDSCAPE WITH
   RED TREES)
   Oil on canvas
   29¼ × 25¼ (inside frame)
   Signature not indicated
   Mills College Art Gallery
   (1925.165)

67. MAGIC MOUNTAINS
   (SUPERSTITION
   MOUNTAINS)
   Oil on board
   30 × 36
   Signed LR
   Monterey Peninsula
   Museum of Art
   Exh. CPLH; perhaps exh.
   LGC, *The Gallery*, March
   1965, No. 16; MEC.
   See Nos. 25, 557 here

68. MARINE-PACIFIC
   OCEAN
   Oil on canvas
   29 × 35
   Signed (location not
   indicated)
   Emma-Rose Layton

69. MARINE-POINT LOBOS
   Oil on canvas
   24 × 28
   Estate signed LL

70. MEXICAN, A PORTRAIT,
   1936
   Oil on panel
   22 × 16½
   Signed LR
   Gyöngy Laky and
   Thomas Layton
   San Francisco Museum of
   Art sticker on back dated
   April 2, 1936. A photograph
   by Ansel Adams exists of
   this work.

180. PESCADERO POINT, *ca.* 1920. (detail), Coll. Molly Jeppson, cat. no. 82.

71. MEXICAN GIRL
    Oil on canvas
    30 × 25
    Signed LL
    City of Carmel-by-the-Sea
    See MPH, July 13, 1962

72. MONTEREY CYPRESS
    Oil on canvas (1939 ?)
    30 × 36
    Signed LR
    Permanent Collection of the Sheldon Swope Art Gallery, Terre Haute, Indiana
    Illus. *Terre Haute Tribune-Star*, Apr. 22, 1979. Exh. CPLH. See n. 336

73. MONTEREY SHORE
    Oil on board
    36 × 40
    Signed LL
    Monterey Peninsula Museum of Art
    Exh. GNG, No. 19; MEC, No. 3; LGC, *The Gallery*, March 1965, No. 28

74. MOUNTAINS AND CANYON IN ARIZONA
    Oil on canvas
    28 × 35
    Signed (location not indicated)
    Emma-Rose Layton

75. NATURAL BRIDGE, *ca.* 1921
    Oil on canvas
    25 × 30
    Estate signed LR

76. NOTLEY'S LANDING, *ca.* 1931
    Oil on canvas
    40 × 51
    Estate signed LL
    Exh. D-WG, 1931

77. OCHRA MOUNTAINS (DESERT MOUNTAINS)
    Oil on canvas
    25 × 30
    Not signed
    Molly Jeppson

78. ORCHARD
    Oil on canvas
    16 × 20
    Authenticated by Emma Pine
    Dr. and Mrs. Sydney T. Wright
    Illus. LGC, *The Gallery*, March 1963, No. 4

79. OLD LADY
    Oil on board
    20 × 16
    Signed LLC
    John Sullivan

80. PALO VERDE, *ca.* 1927
    (Sticker on reverse)
    Oil on canvas
    30 × 36
    Signed LLC
    Norman Mcd. Foster
    Exh. GNG

81. PEAR ORCHARD (WHITE ORCHARD)
    Oil on canvas
    32 × 28
    Authenticated by Emma Pine
    Dr. and Mrs. Sydney T. Wright

82. PESCADERO POINT, *ca.* 1920
    Oil on board
    23 × 29
    Signed LL
    Molly Jeppson

83. PINK MOUNTAIN
    Oil on board
    20 × 24
    Signed LL
    Monterey Peninsula Museum of Art
    Exh. MEC, No. 18

84. POINT LOBOS, CALIFORNIA, *ca.* 1920
    Oil on canvas
    30 × 36
    Signed LR
    Mrs. W. M. Hussey

85. POINT LOBOS FROM PESCADERO POINT
    (Pebble Beach)
    Oil on canvas
    28 × 32
    Signed LL
    Jeannette Parkes Ewing

86. POINT LOBOS TREES
    Oil on canvas
    30 × 36
    Signed LR

87. PORTRAIT OF BEARDED MAN
    Oil on canvas
    30 × 25
    Estate signed UR
    See watercolors Nos. 180, 181 for same sitter. See n. 379

88. PORTRAIT OF MARY FRANCES, *ca.* 1922
    (Mary Frances Hussey)
    Oil on canvas
    30 × 25
    Signed LR
    Jane Johnson

89. PORTRAIT OF MEXICAN WOMAN WITH HAT, *ca.* 1935
    Oil on board
    10¼ × 8¼
    Estate signed LL

90. PORTRAIT OF "POP" HART, 1922
    (George Overbury Hart, Esquire)
    Oil on canvas
    52 × 46
    Signed LR
    Bohemian Club
    Exh. Sixth Annual Exh., Society of Independent Artists, NY, 1922; GNG; CPLH; illus. *Western Woman*, 1951; MEC; Lloyds. See n. 105

91. QUIET SEA
    Oil on canvas
    15½ × 19½
    Signed LR
    Mr. and Mrs. Anthony R. White
    A painting by this title was exh. HGSF, No. 15; Monterey Peninsula Museum of Art, 1976

92. RAGING SEA
    Oil on canvas
    34 × 40
    Estate signed LR

93. RED MOUNTAIN
    Oil on canvas
    36 × 30
    Signed LL
    Dr. and Mrs. Robert J. Tipler
    Exh. as AUTUMN HILLS, CPLH, No. 20; illus. in LGC, *The Gallery*, March 1965, No. 12

94. REDWOOD GLEN
    Oil on canvas
    30 × 36 (approximate)
    Not signed
    Owner anonymous

95. ROCKS AND SEA (SEA AND ROCKS or OCEAN AND ROCK)
    Oil (support not specified)
    19½ × 15
    Signature not reported
    Estate of Donald Winston, James T. Wyman, Executor
    Probably exh. LGC, *The Gallery*, March 1965, No. 27

96. SEA BEYOND THE ROCKS (SEASCAPE)
Oil on canvas
30 × 36
Not signed
Molly Jeppson

97. SEA POOL (POOL)
Oil on canvas
36 × 40
Signed LR
John and Lorna Meyer
Probably exh. D-WG, 1931. See n. 224

98. SEA RHYTHM, ca. 1939 (MAINE COAST; erroneous earlier title)
Oil on canvas
50 × 60
Signed LL
Exh. Golden Gate Intn'l. Expo., SF, 1940 (illustrated)

99. SEASCAPE AND ROCKS, ca. 1939
Oil on canvas
40 × 50
Estate signed LR

100. SEASCAPE; SEA CLOUDS, ca. 1916
Oil on canvas board
9 × 12
Estate signed LR

101. SHADOWS
Oil on canvas
25 × 30
Signed LL

102. SILVER CYPRESS, ca. 1934 (POINT LOBOS)
Oil on canvas
30 × 36
Signed LR
Monterey Peninsula Museum of Art
Descriptions matching this painting were noted in two reviews of the exh. at the CPLH, ns. 105, 258.

103. SNOW SCENE IN HIGH SIERRA
Oil on canvas
24 × 28 (approximate)
Authenticated by Emma Pine
Owner anonymous

104. SOUTH COAST, MONTEREY COUNTY, ca. 1930 (COAST OF CARMEL or COAST SOUTH OF CARMEL)
Oil on canvas
40½ × 44½
Signed LL
Mr. and Mrs. Anthony R. White
Exh. LGC, March 1965, No. 29; illus. in *The Gallery*, March 1965; illus. in MPH, March 18, 1965

105. SPRING LANDSCAPE
Oil on canvas
25 × 30
Not signed
Anne Dickman-Grant

106. SUNSET BUTTE (BUTTE)
Oil on canvas
30 × 36
Signed LR
Anne Dickman-Grant
Exh. GNG, No. 9

107. TAHITIAN (Youth), ca. 1928
Oil on canvas
30 × 25
Signed LL
Discussed in n. 196, along with TAHITIAN YOUTH, PORTRAIT, No. 112 here

108. TAHITIAN BANANAS, ca. 1928 (GREEN BANANAS or BANANA BLOSSOMS)
Oil on canvas
30 × 24½
Signed LCR
Richard Criley
Exh. CPLH

109. TAHITIAN BANANAS NO. 2, ca. 1928
Oil on canvas
46 × 40
Signed LR
A photograph prepared for the 1934 exh. at the CPLH exists. See No. 5 here

BIRD OF PARADISE, ca. 1931, detail of plate 92.

110. TAHITIAN FISH, ca. 1928
Oil on canvas board
15¾ × 19¾
Signed UL
Gyöngy Laky and
Thomas Layton
Exh. D-WG, 1931;
HDMG, 1933; CPLH;
MEC

111. TAHITIAN SCENE,
ca. 1928
Oil on canvas
30 × 36
Signed LLC indistinctly and
estate signed LL.
Description of this or
similar scene in n. 237

112. TAHITIAN YOUTH,
PORTRAIT, ca. 1928
Oil on canvas board
20 × 16
Estate signed UR
Described in n. 196, also
full length painting
TAHITIAN, No. 107 here

113. TAOS LANDSCAPE
(DESERT VILLAGE)
Oil on canvas
25 × 30
Signed LCL
Mr. and Mrs. James F.
Morris
Probably exh. HDMG,
1933; CAA, 1935; Oakland
Art Gallery, 1940, No. 82;
LGC, *The Gallery*, March
1965, No. 14

114. THE MEXICAN
(MEXICAN MAN WITH
HAT AND SERAPE)
Oil on board
24 × 17
Signed LL
William and Brenda Hoot
One of a series of 3 painted
of a "Holy Man" in Mexico.
This work was exh. at LGC,
March 1965, as THE
MEXICAN, No. 4 and was
illus. there as well as in
Carmel Valley Outlook,
Mar. 17, 1965, and MPH,
Oct. 29, 1965. See Nos. 56,
472 here

115. THREE SAGUARO CACTI
(ARIZONA)
Oil on canvas
25½ × 31½
Signed LL
Jane Renner

116. TORMENTED SEA
Oil on canvas
40 × 48
Estate signed LR

117. TOWARD YANKEE
POINT, ca. 1920
Oil on canvas
32 × 40
Signed LLC
Molly Jeppson
Exh. MEC, No. 4

118. TREE IN FIELD
Oil on board
11 × 15½
Authenticated by
Emma Pine
John Sullivan

119. TREES
Oil on canvas
36 × 30
Estate signed LR
Believe these to be
eucalyptus trees.

120. TROPICAL BAY, ca. 1928
Oil on canvas
25 × 30
Not signed
Jane Johnson
Probably Tahiti

121. TROPICAL FISH
(TAHITIAN FISH or
FISH ON A LEAF or
TROPIC FISH)
Oil on board
16 × 20
Signed UL
Molly Jeppson
Exh. CAA, 1934; HDMG,
1933; CPLH; HDMG,
1936, No. 22; MEC

122. UPLAND SOLITUDE,
ca. 1927
(ARIZONA VALLEY)
Oil on canvas
34 × 36
Estate signed LR
A number of critiques
describe this scene well,
e.g., ns. 203, 237. Exh.
GNG, No. 7

123. VALDEZ, ca. 1930
(HILLSIDE VILLAGE or
MEXICAN VILLAGE or
NEW MEXICAN
VILLAGE or TOWN
OF VALDEZ)
Oil on canvas
25 × 30
Signed LL
Exh. CPLH, No. 18; Nelson
Gallery, Kansas City, 1937.
See. n. 154

124. VEILED MOUNTAIN,
ca. 1915
(PAJARO VALLEY)
Oil on board
19½ × 23¼
Signed LR
Temporarily thought to
be Pájaro Valley near
Watsonville, Calif., a work
by that title exh. at GNG,
No. 20, but is certainly
earlier painting and fits
description of VEILED
MOUNTAIN in 1915.
See n. 47

125. VILLAGE SCENE
(MEXICAN VILLAGE or
HAWAIIAN VILLAGE)
Oil on canvas
30 × 36
Estate signed LR

126. VIOLENCE
Oil on composition board
32 × 40
Estate signed LL

127. WILDCAT COVE
Oil on canvas
26 × 32
Not signed
Mrs. W. M. Hussey
Illus. as WILDERNESS
COVE, *Terre Haute
Tribune-Star*, Sept. 12,
1982

128. WINTER SCENE
Oil on canvas
29 × 35
Not signed
Anne Dickman-Grant
Exh. LGC, *The Gallery*,
March 1965, No. 17

WATERCOLORS

129. A LANDSCAPE GARNER
[sic]
17½ × 11½
Estate signed LR

130. ALICE IN
WONDERLAND
RABBIT, ca. 1920
24 × 20
Not signed
Molly Jeppson

131. BEARDED MAN,
BANANA GROVE, ca. 1928
(OLD MAN WITH
BANANA FRUITS)
22 × 18
Estate signed UL

132. BIG TREE
20 × 15
Signed LL

133. BLUE COVE AND
PARCHED HILLS, 1938
20½ × 30
Signed LR and dated
Monterey Peninsula
Museum of Art
Indistinctly dedicated: To
Turzak and Juliet [?]

134. BLUE COVE, DARK
CLIFFS
8⅝ × 11¾
Estate signed LR

135. BOWL OF FRUIT
(ABSTRACT)
14 × 11
Not signed (acquired from
artist)
Russell Williams

136. BRILLIANT COVE
12 × 16
Estate signed LL

137. BROWN PROMONTORY
15 × 19⅝
Signed LR

138. CLOUD OVER HAWAII,
1934
15 × 18
Signed (location not
indicated) and dated.
Purchased from artist in
1937
William Henry Black

139. COAST RANGE
19½ × 25½
Estate signed LL
Framed as diptych with
No. 203

140. COAST ROCKS AND SEA
18⅞ × 24⅞
Estate signed LR
Very similar to CORSAIR, oil painting No. 28

141. COASTAL SCENE
15 × 22
Not signed
Jane Johnson

142. COLORFUL SURF, *ca.* 1916
10 × 14
Signed LR

143. COVE AND BATHERS, *ca.* 1916
10 × 12¼
Signed LR
The Fieldstone Company

144. CYPRESS AND OCEAN
Watercolor on "parchment"
(Perhaps this is the Formica-like material mentioned on p. 85.)
20 × 27
Signed LL
Mrs. W. M. Hussey

145. CYPRESS AND SEA
22 × 18
Estate signed LC

146. CYPRESS TRUNKS AND FOREST
22¼ × 29⅝
Estate signed LL

147. CYPRESSES AND TURQUOISE SKY
22⅝ × 15⅛
Estate signed LR

148. DUNES AND TRUNKS
18 × 22
Estate signed LL

149. EARTH AND SEA
21 × 27
Signed LR
William and Grace Davis

150. EQUINE FRIEND
19½ × 19
Estate signed LR

151. FISH
26½ × 36
Signature not reported
The Hugh Lane Municipal Gallery of Modern Art
See n. 238

152. FISHER WIVES
3⅜ × 4¾
Signed LL
Gyöngy Laky and Thomas Layton
Illus. LGC, *The Gallery*, March 1965; cover of *The Gallery*, March 1969

153. FLAVINS' HOUSE AT CACHAGUA; OUTSIDE BAR, *ca.* 1940
21 × 24
Dedication: "To the most hospitable Señor O'Flavin on his birthday, November Two. The Redwood bar at Cachagua hacienda (signed) John"
Sean Flavin

154. GHOST FOREST, 1934
Watercolor on Formica
16 × 20
Signed LR and dated
Label on reverse: CAA

155. GHOST TREE
17½ × 21½
Not signed
John Sullivan

156. GOAT
18 × 16¾
Estate signed CR

157. GRAY SHAWL
22¾ × 15¼
Estate signed CR

158. GREEN COVE, RED SLOPE, *ca.* 1916
9¾ × 13¾
Signed LR

159. GREEN-BLUE WATERS
11⅞ × 17⅛
Estate signed LC

160. HE AND SHE
18 × 23
Estate signed LC

161. HEART OF CYPRESS AT CLIFF
22 × 29½
Signed LR

162. HIGHLANDS COAST
15 × 20
Estate signed LL

163. HILLS, FURROWS AND TRUNK
15⅛ × 10⅞
Signed LC

164. HUNGRY GOAT
13½ × 16⅜
Estate signed LR

181. GOAT, cat. no. 156.

165. IN THE WOODS
22⅝ × 15⅜
Estate signed UR

166. LANDSCAPE
Watercolor
8⅜ × 6¼
Estate signed LR
On reverse of announcement to artists for 1933 Annual Exhibition (March 5–April 9), Oakland Art Gallery. Work to be submitted "not later than February 25th."

167. LEDA IN REPOSE
(Police dog)
18 × 20
Estate signed LL
See text p. 88. Believe this to be the work exh. as a charcoal at CPLH, No. 42.

168. MARKET SCENE, MEXICO (MEXICAN MARKET)
8 × 11½
Not signed
Molly Jeppson
Exh. HDMG, 1940, No. 3; MEC, No. 27.

169. NEAR TAOS, *ca.* 1930
10 × 12¾
Signed LR

170. OCEAN THROUGH TREES; POINT LOBOS, CALIFORNIA
23 × 29
Estate signed LL

171. OCEAN WAVES
13½ × 9½
Signed LL
Acquired from artist
Russell Williams

172. OLD TRUNKS
30³⁄₁₆ × 22½
Signed LR

173. OPALESCENT COAST
9⁵⁄₁₆ × 14
Signed LL

174. OVERLOOKING COVE
16 × 23
Not signed
Molly Knox

175. THE PEAK, *ca.* 1934 (FANTASY I)
Watercolor on Formica
15 × 19 (sight)
Signed LR
See review of CPLH exh. in n. 258

176. POINT LOBOS
(Turquoise pool)
15 × 20
Estate signed LL

177. POISED
Artist's title on reverse
15⅛ × 22½
Signed LR
See comments in n. 338

178. POISED NO. 2
19 × 25
Estate signed LL

179. PORTRAIT; BALD MAN
WITH RED NOSE
16¼ × 10⅝
Estate signed UR

180. PORTRAIT; BEARDED
MAN
30½ × 22⅝
Estate signed LR
See Nos. 87, 181.

181. PORTRAIT; BEARDED
MAN
26¼ × 20⅜
Estate signed LR
Same as No. 180 but with
table lamp in background.
See also No. 87

182. PORTRAIT; BEARDED
MAN IN GREEN
10¼ × 8¼
Estate signed LL

183. PORTRAIT; MAN WITH
RED TIE
30½ × 22⅝
Estate signed LL

184. PORTRAIT; MEXICAN
GIRL
Watercolor on board
17 × 13
Not signed
Molly Jeppson

185. PORTRAIT; A
MINNESOTA HANSON
(A country gentleman)
14 × 11
Not signed
Dr. and Mrs. Sydney T.
Wright
Exh. MEC, No. 28

186. PORTRAIT; OLD MAN,
TEAL BLUE
9⅞ × 6
Estate signed LL

187. PORTRAIT; WHITE-
HAIRED MAN
18 × 17½
Estate signed UR

188. PORTRAIT; WOMAN IN
APRON
30½ × 23¼
Signed LR

189. PORTRAIT; WOMAN IN
BLACK
19¾ × 15⅛
Signed LR

190. PROFILE
8⅛ × 5⅛
Estate signed LL

191. PURPLE TREE, FALL
14¼ × 11¼
Estate signed LL

192. PURPLE TREE, FALL
NO. 2
18 × 22
Estate signed UR

193. RABBIT ISLAND OFF
OAHU, HAWAII, ca. 1930
11 × 15
Estate signed LL

194. RED ROCKS BY THE
SEA
16 × 20⅛
Estate signed LR
Gordon and Joan Spencer

195. RED-BROWN HILLS,
BLUE MOUNTAINS
19½ × 25½
Estate signed LL

196. REDWOOD BASES
21 × 18
Estate signed LL

197. REDWOOD TREES
Watercolor on Formica
21 × 15
Signed LL
Mrs. W. M. Hussey

198. ROCK AND FOAM
9⅝ × 13¼
Signed LC

199. ROCK PEAKS AND SURF
9¾ × 13½
Estate signed LL

200. ROCKS AND SWIRLS,
ca. 1916
9¼ × 12½
Signed LR

201. SAN XAVIER DE BAC
MISSION, ca. 1930
(CHURCH AT TUCSON)
11 × 17
Not signed
Molly Jeppson

202. SAND KING
22¾ × 15
Signed LR

203. SANTA CRUZ HILLS
19½ × 25½
Estate signed LL
Framed as diptych with
No. 139

204. SEA TREE
17¾ × 11⅞
Estate signed LR

205. SEASCAPE
13½ × 16½
Signed LL
Gordon and Joan Spencer

206. SEASCAPE
22⅞ × 30⅝
Estate signed LL

207. SHORELINE AND
COAST HILLS
THROUGH ROCKS
30 × 22¼
Estate signed LR

208. STORKS
22 × 18
Estate signed UL

209. TAHITI SHORES, ca. 1928
(TROPICAL ISLE)
10½ × 14½
Not signed
Molly Jeppson

210. TIDE POOL
13¾ × 17¾
Estate signed LL

211. TIDE POOLS, RED
HILL, ca. 1916
11½ × 14¾
Estate signed LR

212. TROPICAL FOLIAGE,
ca. 1928
14 × 20
Estate signed LC

213. TRUNK, ROCK, SAND
AND SEA
19¾ × 25⅝
Estate signed LC

214. TRUNKS AND ROUGH
SEA
24¼ × 18
Estate signed LR

215. TURQUOISE BAY
15 × 20
Estate signed LL

CHARCOALS

216. ABSTRACTION:
GEOMETRICS (NO. 1),
ca. 1933
22½ × 17½
Signed LR

217. ABSTRACTION:
GEOMETRICS (NO. 2),
ca. 1933
22¾ × 17½
Signed LC

218. ABSTRACTION:
GEOMETRICS (NO. 3),
ca. 1933
21½ × 17½
Signed LL

219. ABSTRACTION: GRAVEN
SANDSTONE (NO. 1),
ca. 1933
21½ × 18¾
Estate signed UL

220. ABSTRACTION: GRAVEN
SANDSTONE (NO. 2),
ca. 1933
19⅝ × 17½
Signed LC
Exh. CAA. See CPC,
Oct. 19, 1934

221. ABSTRACTION: LEAVES
18 × 15¼
Estate signed LL

222. ABSTRACTION: STONES
AND BRANCHES
18¾ × 23⅞
Estate signed LL

223. AFRICAN STATUE
23 × 17¾
Signed LL
Probably exh. D-WG, 1933

224. BARNYARD ROOSTER,
ca. 1930
(COCK)
22 × 17½
Signed LCR
Richard Criley
Exh. D-WG, 1933; CPLH,
No. 55

225. CARICATURE; BIG NOSE
9½ × 7⅞
Estate signed LR

226. CHINESE COOK
20 × 16
Signed LR
Mrs. George H. Macy

227. CITYSCAPE
22¾ × 19 (sight)
Estate signed LC
See discussion n. 354.
Probably exh. D-WG, 1945.
See No. 363 here

228. COLOURMAN, *ca.* 1933
(NOCTURNE)
21 × 17
Signed (location not
reported)
The Hugh Lane Municipal
Gallery of Modern Art
Exh. CPLH. See n. 238

229. DANCER AND ROCKS
(NO. 1)
23⅞ × 18⅝
Estate signed LR

230. DANCER AND ROCKS
(NO. 2)
23⅞ × 18¾
Estate signed LL

231. FOAM AND ROCKS
16¼ × 19½
Estate signed LR

232. GIRL EATING
17⅛ × 16½
Signed LR
Exh. James Vigeveno
Galleries, Los Angeles
(label), 1953; CAA, 1955
(label). See n. 368

232. A GIRL EATING
17⅛ × 16½
Signed LR
Exh. James Vigeveno
Galleries, Los Angeles
(label), 1953; CAA, 1955
(label). See n. 368
See p. 134 for discussion

233. PORTRAIT; MAN IN
WOODS
23¾ × 18¾
Estate signed LL

234. ROCK SURFACE
17½ × 21½
Estate signed UL

235. SEA AND ROCKS
18⅝ × 23½
Estate signed LL

236. SLEEPING DOGS
ca. 22 × 17½
Estate signed LR

237. SMOOTH, DEEP CLIFF
18½ × 22⅝
Estate signed LR

238. STROLLER
23 × 17½
Estate signed UL

239. SWIRLING WATER,
ROUND ROCK
18 × 23 (sight)
Signed LL

240. TREE BARK
(OLD CYPRESS TRUNK)
18 × 23
Signed (location not
reported)
The Hugh Lane Municipal
Gallery of Modern Art
Exh. CPLH. See n. 238

241. TREE GROWING OUT
OF STONE
(STUDY OF TREES AND
ROCKS)
22 × 18
Not signed
Emma-Rose Layton

242. VORTEX
23½ × 18¾
Signed LC
Probably CPLH, No. 57;
LGC label. See n. 234

243. WAVES ON ROCKS
19 × 24 (sight)
Estate signed LR
LGC label

244. WHITE BOULDER AND
TREE
23¾ × 18⅝
Estate signed LL

245. WHITE INLETS
18½ × 23¼
Estate signed LL

246. YEARLING
11 × 17¾
Estate signed LR

CRAYON

247. MAN WITH MEXICAN
HAT, *ca.* 1935
9¼ × 6⅛
Estate signed LR

248. NURSING MOTHER
8⅛ × 11
Estate signed LC

249. OLIVE TREES,
MAJORCA, NO. 1
18¾ × 23⅞
Signed LC (titled and
located)

250. OLIVE TREES,
MAJORCA, NO. 2
20 × 25½
Estate signed LC

251. PIG AND PIGLETS
10 × 7½
Signed LL
Given by artist to Mrs.
Criley, *ca.* 1940–1945
Russell Williams

252. PORTRAIT: JEB
CASSIDY (?)
12¼ × 11
Estate signed LL

253. PORTRAIT: PROFILE
OF MAN
11⅞ × 8⅝
Estate signed LR

254. PRAYERS
9⅛ × 6⅛
Estate signed LL

255. RED ROCKS
18⅛ × 23⅛
Estate signed LR

256. SOW
7⅛ × 11⅝
Signed LR

CHARCOAL AND WATERCOLOR

257. FLIGHT INTO EGYPT
12¾ × 17¾
Estate signed LR

258. FOAM, ROCKS AND
COAST
18¼ × 22½
Estate signed LL

259. MEXICAN
SALESWOMAN, *ca.* 1935
(BLUE LADY)
15 × 11
Not signed
Molly Jeppson
Exh. CAA, 1945. See
Nos. 296, 297 here

260. SEA CREATURE
(YOUNG OTTER)
17 × 23¼
Estate signed LL

261. TROPICAL FRUIT
24 × 20
Signed LR
Molly Jeppson
Possibly done in Tahiti or
Hawaii

CHARCOAL AND CONTE CRAYON

262. CALM BAY
18¼ × 22¼
Estate signed LR

263. HEADS
23½ × 17½
Signed LR
LGC label. Perhaps No. 21
in LGC, March 1965 exh.
titled NATIVE WOMEN

264. LONELY TREE
(CYPRESS ON ROCKS)
18 × 13 (sight)
Signed LR

265. MONTEREY CYPRESS
23 × 18½
Signed LL
Richard Criley
Gift from artist in late 1940s
or early 1950s

266. PORTRAIT: MAN WITH
MOUSTACHE
18½ × 17
Estate signed LR
Illegible inscription UR

267. ROCKS AND STUMP
23¼ × 18¾
Estate signed LR

268. WINDSWEPT ROCK
24 × 17¼
Signed LL

182. PORTRAIT: RED HEAD, BLUE EYES, cat. no. 278. Photographer unknown.

MIXED MEDIA

269. CALIFORNIA LANDSCAPE
7¾ × 10¾
Signed LL
Helen Christensen

270. CLOSING HOUR
22 × 18
Signed LR
Exh. MEC, No. 21

271. DEEP CHASM
18⅞ × 23⅞
Estate signed LL

272. DONKEY
16 × 9
Estate signed LL

273. LEAFLESS
18 × 22
Estate signed LL

274. MAN IN ARM CHAIR
15¾ × 11
Signed LR

275. PORTRAIT: BLUE BOW TIE
14¼ × 11¾
Estate signed LR

276. PORTRAIT: OPALESCENT
11⅜ × 9⅜
Estate signed LL

277. PORTRAIT: RED HEAD WOMAN
12¼ × 11
Estate signed LR

278. PORTRAIT: RED HEAD, BLUE EYES
12 × 14¾
Signed LR

279. PORTRAIT: RED LIPS
16½ × 13½
Estate signed LR

280. PORTRAIT: RED MOUSTACHE
17¾ × 12¼
Estate signed LR

281. PORTRAIT: RED NOSE (BLACK BART)
11¾ × 8¾
Estate signed LR

282. PORTRAIT: WOMAN IN BLUE
11⅝ × 9¾
Estate signed UL

283. PORTRAIT: YOUNGSTER IN PINK AND BLUE
16¾ × 11⅝
Estate signed LL

284. SEATED MAN
15⅞ × 11
Estate signed LR
Exh. MEC, No. 26

285. TREES AND ROCKS
24 × 19
Inscribed UL: "John O'Shea to John Garrett Williams, May 26, 1941"
John Garrett Williams

286. WHITE POOL
18½ × 23¼
Estate signed LL

OTHER

287. RUGGED COAST
Charcoal and ink
18⅞ × 24¼
Estate signed LR

288. CYPRESS TRUNK
Gouache
29 × 22¾
Estate signed LR

289. BABY BURRO
Crayon and watercolor
4⅛ × 6
Signed LL
Monterey Peninsula Museum of Art
Exh. HDMG, 1936, No. 19

290. MEXICAN VILLAGE
Watercolor and graphite
12 × 17
Signed LL (written signature, probably early painting)
Molly Jeppson

291. PORTRAIT: OLD MAN, ca. 1934
Watercolor and graphite on Formica
4⅛ × 4
Signed LR
Penciled dedication on reverse
Dan James (belonged to father "D. L.")

292. HUMAN FIGURES
Lithographic drawing
18⅝ × 18 (sight)
Signature not indicated
Mills College Art Gallery (1934.43)

293. POISED
Lithographic print
9¼ × 10
Estate signed LR

294. ABSTRACTION: COAST
Graphite
18 × 22
Estate signed UL

295. NATIVE CHILDREN
Graphite
17½ × 11¾
Signed LR

296. WOMAN IN SHAWL
Graphite
9½ × 15¾
Estate signed LL
This drawing and No. 297 appear to be preliminary studies for No. 259 here.

297. WOMEN IN SHAWLS
Graphite
15⅜ × 22⅝
Estate signed LC
See Nos. 259, 296 here

298. CYPRESS
Etching
10 × 7
Not signed
Jane Johnson

299. CYPRESSES AT COVE
Etching
4 × 7
Signed in plate and LL
(First proof)

300. CYPRESS GROVE
Etching
6 × 4
Not signed
Jane Johnson

301. LOBOS
Etching
6 × 8
Signed in plate and LR

302. LONE TREE
Etching
2⅞ × 2⅛
Signed LR in plate

303. MEXICAN VILLAGE
Etching
6 × 8
Signed LL

304. MONTEREY PINE
Etching
8 × 6
Signed in plate and LR

305. STILLWATER COVE
Etching
6⅛ × 8
Signed in plate LL

306. GEORGE BERNARD SHAW, ca. 1931
Stone, cut-direct
ca. 24 tall × 10 × 10
D. Kirke Erskine
See text p. 65 for discussion

II. UNLOCATED WORKS

In this section, we list alphabetically unlocated works by a recorded title and the source of information. Where available, further information is given. Because title changes are known to have occurred, we assume that there are some duplications of entries not only within this section but between this and the preceding section listing known works. This problem could not be resolved, but inadvertent duplication was offset by avoiding exclusion.

307. ABALONE POINT
Painting
HGSF, No. 21

308-314. ABSTRACTIONS NOS. 1–7
Charcoal
D-WG, 1933; MPH, Feb. 14, 1933; MPH, Mar. 9, 1933

315-319. ABSTRACTIONS NOS. 34, 38, 40, 51, 59
Charcoal
CPLH

320. AFTER THE STORM ("Japanesque")
Watercolor
HDMG, 1940

321. AGATE MOUNTAIN
Watercolor
SFAA, 1936, No. 65; HDMG, 1936, No. 25; HDMG, 1940, No. 9

322. AGED HARMONY
Watercolor
HDMG, 1940, No. 2; MPH, Sept. 24, 1940

323. ALONG THE COAST
22L

324. ALONG THE SHORE
Probably an oil painting
CPC, Oct. 12, 1934

325. AN ACTIVE SEA
Painting
HGSF, No. 7

326. AN ADOBE (NEW MEXICAN ADOBE)
1931E; HDMG, 1933

327. AN AFTERNOON CALL
Painting
HDMG, 1936, No. 13

328. ANCIENT MONARCH
Watercolor
HDMG, 1940

329. ANCIENT OAK
Probably charcoal
Controversy, Nov. 2, 1934
Albert M. Bender Collection

330. ANCIENT OAK
Watercolor
HDMG, 1940, No. 7

331. AN ELFIN FOREST
Painting
HGSF, No. 12

332. ANEMONE BAY
Painting
HGSF, No. 10

333. APACHE STRONGHOLD
Painting
GNG, No. 2; LAT, Feb. 5, 1928

334. THE API
1931E

335. APPLES
Oil painting
FMC

336. ARCADY POPLARS
FMC; LAT, May 9, 1915

337. ARIZONA CACTUS
1931E

338. ARIZONA MOUNTAIN
Oil painting
HWWL

339. ARIZONA MOUNTAINS
Oil painting
25 × 30
MEC

340. ARIZONA'S OBELISKS-THE SAHUAROS
Painting
GNG, No. 14

341. ATLANTIC MARINE
Painting
CPLH, No. 22

342. AT MASS
Painting
HDMG, 1936, No. 15; CPC, July 31, 1936

343. ATOL [sic] OF THE SUN
HDMG, 1933; MPH, Sept. 14, 1933

344. AT SUNSET
Painting
HGSF, No. 6

345. AT THE RISING MOON
D-WG, probably 1931

346. AUTUMN
Oil
FMC

347. AUTUMN HILLS
Painting
CPLH, No. 26

348. AUTUMN ON THE HUDSON
Probably an oil painting
22L; CPC, Oct. 12, 1934

349. AXTEC WOMAN
CAA (year ?)

350. THE BALLET
Oil
FMC; LAT, May 9, 1915

351. BARTENDER
Charcoal
SAG

352. BEACH SANDS
Oil
FMC

353. BEBEDOR (MUCHO MESCAL)
Painting
HDMG, 1936, No. 1; CPC, July 31, 1936

354. BEFORE THE LEAP
Painting
HGSF, No. 2

355. BEGGAR
Painting
18 × 24
HDMG, 1936, No. 3; MEC, No. 25

356. BIG SUR
Painting
KG, No. 7

357. BIG SUR COUNTRY
Painting
SAG; CPLH, No. 28

358. BLACK VASE
Charcoal
D-WG, 1933

359. BLEACHED MESA
Painting
CPLH, No. 27

360. BLUE LAGOON
Painting (?)
HDMG, 1940

361. BRUGH OF ANGUS
Oil painting
FMC

362. BUNNY
CAA (year ?)

363. BUSINESS SECTION CARMEL (an abstraction)
Probably charcoal
CAA, 1945. Perhaps CITYSCAPE. See No. 227 here

364. CACTUS GARDEN
Oil painting
CPLH, No. 61

365. CALIFORNIA COAST
Painting (?)
HDMG, 1940

366. CALIORENCI COAST (?)
SAG

367. CAMPO DE ORO
Painting
GNG, No. 16

368. CARLOTTA
Watercolor
HDMG, 1936, No. 8; CPC, July 31, 1936; HDMG, 1940

369. CARMEL
Painting
HGSF, No. 9; Lloyds

370. CARMEL BLUE
Painting
KG, No. 18

371. CARMEL HIGHLANDS
KG, added to catalogue as No. 28

372. CARTOUCHE
Charcoal
D-WG, 1933; CPLH, No. 53

373. CATHEDRAL
Oil painting
FMC; LAT, May 9, 1915

374. CHILD'S HEAD (a smaller canvas)
CAA; CPC, Nov. 23, 1934

375. CHINESE CHILD
CAA (year ?)

376. CHRISTOPHERO
Probably an oil painting
HDMG, 1936, No. 12; CAA (year ?)

377. CHUNAUAN (?)
Charcoal
D-WG, 1933

378. CLEARING MISTS
Painting
HDMG, 1936, No. 24

379. CLOSING HOUR
Probably a paper work (chalk?)
MEC, No. 21

380. COAST GUARDS
Oil painting
FMC

381. COCONUT PALMS
1931E

382. COCONUT PALMS AT EDGE OF WATER
Ella Winter, *Carmelite*, April 3, 1929

383. COLT
Painting
CAA, 1945. See n. 354

384. COMPAÑEROS
(TWO STANDING MEN)
Painting
HDMG, 1936, No. 5

385. CON MUCHO GUSTO
Painting
HDMG, 1936, No. 11;
CAA (year ?)

386. CORMORANT ROOKERY
Painting
HGSF, No. 8

387. CORRAL DE TIERRA
Painting
GNG, No. 27

388. COVE
CAA; CPC, Aug. 26, 1938

389. COVE OF JADE
Painting
HGSF, No. 22

390. CRAGS
FMC; LAT, May 9, 1915

391. CYPRESS GROVE
Painting
KG, No. 5

392. CYPRESS GROVE
Painting
GNG, No. 23; D-WG, 1931

393. DESERT HILLS
(Panorama under vast sky)
Probably an oil painting
HGP

394. DESERT NEAR TUCSON
Painting
GNG, No. 12

395. DESERT NIGHT
(Probably small painting)
CAA; CPC, Dec. 10, 1937

396. DEVIL'S CAULDRON
Painting
HGSF, No. 16

397. DIM HORIZON
Painting
KG, No. 20

398. DON QUIXOTE
Pastel (?)
9½ × 12
MEC, No. 29; HWWL

399. DRIVING RAIN ON GROVE OF TREES
Probably an oil painting
HGP

400. DWARF
Painting
HDMG, 1936, No. 16

401. EARLY SPRING
Oakland Art Gallery, 1939, No. 67

402. EBON REEFS
Probably small oil painting
SFAA, 1918, No. 232

403. EL PALO COLORADO
Painting
KG, No. 4

404. ENCROACHING SHADOWS
Painting
KG, No. 19

405. EUCALYPTI
Oil painting
FMC; *Graphic*, Feb. 3, 1915, p. 13

406. EUCALYPTI
Painting
LAMA, 1920, No. 31
Lent by Miss Augusta Senter

407. EURASIAN LADY
Charcoal
CAA; CPC, Oct. 19, 1934;
D-WG, 1933; CPLH, No. 39

408. FLAMBOYANT
Probably an oil painting
SAG; HDMG, 1933; MPH, Sept. 14, 1933

409. FLOWER PAINTING (A TROPICAL)
(a smaller canvas)
CAA; CPC, Nov. 23, 1934

410. FLOWERS
Oil painting (?)
LGC, *The Gallery*, March 1965, No. 32

411. FRIENDLY COUNTRY
Painting
KG, No. 9

412. GAP
Probably an oil painting
44th Annual Exh. of the SFAA, 1920

413. GOAT
Charcoal
Mrs. Douglas Short
D-WG, 1933; MPH, Mar. 9, 1933; CPLH, No. 49

414. GOAT WHAT ATE THE SANDS
Watercolor (?)
CAA, 1945. See n. 354

415. GOING HOME FROM MARKET
(Mexican painting purchased by collector to be placed in the Chicago Art Institute, but not there 1984)
Game and Gossip, 1952.
See n.7

416. GOLDEN HILLTOP
Painting
HGSF, No. 4

417. GOLDEN MESCAL
Painting
KG, No. 8

418. GOOD MORROW
Oil painting
FMC

419. GOTHIC HEAD
Watercolor
CAA, 1945

420. GREEN GRASS
Oil painting
FMC

421. HAWAII (HAWAIIAN LANDSCAPE)
Probably an oil painting
25 × 30
HDMG, 1933; CPLH, No. 11; CAA; CPC, Sept. 16, 1938; MEC, No. 15; HWWL; Maybe "Brickman" show, 1946. See No. 422 here

422. HAWAIIAN LANDSCAPE
Oil painting
1931E; HDMG, 1933; CPLH; reproduced MPH, Nov. l, 1946. See No. 421 here

423. HAWAIIAN LANDSCAPE
MPH, Sept. 14, 1933; HDMG, 1933

424. HAWAII SUMMER HILLS
(Maybe OAHU HILLS ?)
Probably an oil painting
CAA; CPC, July 29, 1938

425. HEAD
Charcoal
CPLH, No. 24

426. HEAD MAN OF THE VILLAGE
(A Mexican study)
See n. 113
Albert M. Bender Collection

427. HEAD MEXICAN
"Small Pastel"
HWWL

428. HEAVY SURF
Painting
KG, No. 14

429. HERMIT
Painting
HDMG, 1936, No. 2

430. HIGH BLOOD PRESSURE
D-WG, 1933

431. HIGH HAT
Painting
HDMG, 1936, No. 17

432. HIGHLANDS CLIFFS
Watercolor
HDMG, 1940, No. 4

433. HIGH TIDE
Painting
HGSF, No. 11

434. HILLSIDE IN TOPANGA
Oil painting
FMC

435. HOME FRONT
(Depicting a bird)
Watercolor (?)
CAA, 1945. See n. 354

436. HORSE MESA
Probably an oil painting
GNG, No. 3; Temple Art Gallery, Tucson, 1928; Beaux Arts Galerie, San Francisco, 1928; Nelson Gallery, Kansas City, 1937; CAA; CPC, Nov. 12, 1937

437. IN A TREMOR
Painting
KG, No. 27

438. IN AUTUMN RAIMENT
(Maine?)
Painting
KG, No. 23. See n. 35

439. AN IMPORTANT
LITTLE MAN
Watercolor
HDMG, 1940, No. 10

440. INDIAN GIRL
Charcoal
D-WG, 1933; CPLH,
No. 48

441. INDIAN MAN
(Possibly New Mexican)
Watercolor
18 × 12 (memory sight)
Seen in Berkeley 1960
(courtesy Paul Carey)

442. INDIAN YOUTH
(INDIAN BUCK)
Painting
HDMG, 1933 (?); CPLH,
No. 25

443. IN THE REDWOODS
Painting
HGSF, No. 13

444. ITSELF
Oil painting
FMC

445. KANEOHE BAY
Painting
CPLH, No. 2

446. KELP GARDEN
Charcoal
CPLH, No. 33

447. LADY BACON
Charcoal
D-WG, 1933

448. LAGUNA
Painting
LAMA, 1920, No. 30
Lent by Miss Augusta
Senter

449. LAND OF A THOUSAND
SMOKES
(Alaska ?)
Watercolor
HDMG, 1940, No. 5.
See n. 338

450. LAND OF THE
FORTY-NINERS
Painting
KG, No. 1; Lloyds

451. LAND OF WONDER
Painting
GNG, No. 10; LAT, Feb. 5,
1928

452. LANDSCAPE
Painting
LAMA, 1921, No. 42
Lent by Miss Augusta
Senter

453. LANDSCAPE
Watercolor
CPLH, No. 63

454. LANDSCAPE
Watercolor
LGC, 1965, No. 7

455. LANDSCAPE FROM
STUDIO WINDOW,
TAXCO
Watercolor
CAA, 1945; MPH, June 14,
1945

456. LAUGHING WOMAN
Chalk or gouache (?)
CAA, 1945

457. LAVA SCUPLTURE
Charcoal
CPLH, No. 46

458. LILIES
Charcoal
D-WG, 1933

459. LISA CONCHA
Painting
CPLH, No. 17

460. LITTLE TREE THAT
LOST ITS HEAD
Painting
KG, No. 21

461. LOBOS HEADLAND
Painting
HGSF, No. 17

462. LONE TREE
Oil painting
Not signed
Illus. LGC, *The Gallery*,
March 1965

463. MADAME BUNNY
Oil painting
CPLH, No. 60

464. MAINE COAST
(Description)
(SEASCAPE ?) (dated
1921 ?)
Oil painting(s)
30 × 36 (?)
D-WG, 1934; MPH, Oct.
6, 1934; E.B. Crocker Art
Gallery, Sacramento, 1935;
KG, No. 24; D-WG, 1931;
CPC, Sept. 16, 1938; MEC,
No. 16; CPC, Oct. 12,
1934; CPC, Feb. 11, 1938;
LGC, *The Gallery*, March
1965, No. 30; Nelson
Gallery, Kansas City, 1937;
Lloyds. Perhaps several
works

465. MANANNAAN'S THRONE
Probably an oil painting
SFAA, 1918, No. 231;
HGSF, No. 3

466. MAN IN A STOVE PIPE
HAT, ca. 1940
Charcoal
Albert M. Bender
Collection

467. MARADA [sic]
(Maybe same as
PENITENTE MARADA,
No. 508)
Oil painting
Signed LR
Cover illus. LGC, *The
Gallery*, March 1965,
No. 20

468. MARINE
Oil
FMC

469. MARINE
"Small watercolor"
CAA (year ?)

470. MAY WONG
HDMG, 1933

471. MEDITATION
Painting
HDMG, 1936, No. 20

472. MEXICAN
Oil painting
LGC, *The Gallery*, March
1965, No. 24—not to be
confused with THE
MEXICAN, No. 4. See
No. 114 here

473. MEXICAN DRAMA
HWWL, oil; MEC, No. 24,
a paper work (?); LGC,
The Gallery, March 1965,
No. 8, oil (?)

474. MEXICAN GIRL
Oakland Art Gallery, 1939,
No. 69

475. MEXICAN HEAD
Paper work (?)
11 × 12
HWWL; MEC, No. 23

476. MEXICAN LANDSCAPE
Painting
1931E; HDMG, 1936,
No. 27; CAA (year ?)

477. MEXICAN HASH [sic]
WASH WOMAN
Painting
HDMG, 1936, No. 21; CAA
(year ?)

478. MEXICAN WOMAN
Watercolor
CAA, 1945; MPH, June 14,
1945
Mrs. D. L. James (in 1945)

479. MIXED FLOWERS
Oil painting
28 × 32
HWWL; 22L; HDMG,
1933; E.B. Crocker Art
Gallery, Sacramento, Mar.
4, 1935 (paper ?); CAA
(year ?); MEC, No. 19

480. MONHEGAN, MAINE
Painting
GNG, No. 28; LAT, Feb. 5,
1928; sales receipt from
Carmel Valley Art Gallery,
n.d.

481. MOONLIGHT
Painting
HGSF, No. 1; KG, No. 10;
Lloyds; GNG, No. 24;
HDMG, 1940. See No. 547
here

482. MOSS LANDING SALT
WORKS
Oil painting
32 × 40
MEC, No. 6

483. MOSSY ROCKS
Oil painting
FMC

484. MOUNTAIN
Charcoal
D-WG, 1933

485. MOUNTAIN VILLAGE
Painting
HDMG, 1936, No. 18

486. NATIVE WOMEN
Oil painting (?)
LGC, *The Gallery*, March
1965, No. 21

487. NEWLY-CUT ROAD THROUGH HILLS NEAR PASADENA
Probably an oil painting
HGP

488. NEW MEXICAN DESERT
1931E

489. NEW MEXICAN LANDSCAPE
(Probably PAPAGO TERRITORY)
Painting
HDMG, 1933; CPLH, No. 23

490. NIGHT BLOOMING CEREUS
Oil painting
D-WG, 1934; CPLH, No. 29; *Controversy*, Nov. 2, 1934

491. NIGHT FOLK
FMC; LAT, May 9, 1915

492. NOCTURNE
D-WG, 1933; CPLH, No. 47, charcoal; HDMG, 1936, painting

493. NOVEMBER
Painting (Maine?)
KG, No. 26. See n. 35

494. OCTOBER
Painting (Maine?)
KG, No. 25. See n. 35

495. OLDEST INHABITANTS
Painting
KG, No. 3

496. OLDEST NATIVE
Probably an oil painting
HWWL

497. OLDEST NATIVE
Watercolor
HDMG, 1940; MPH, Sept. 24, 1940

498. OLD TREES
Painting
HDMG, 1936, No. 26

499. OLD TREES, MONTEREY
Oakland Art Gallery, 1939, No. 68

500. OLD WOMAN
HDMG, 1936
(added to "program")

501. PALI
D-WG, 1931; CPLH, No. 4; Nelson Gallery, Kansas City, 1937; Oakland Art Gallery, 1940, No. 81. See n. 203

502. PAN'S ACRE
Painting
KG, No. 13; Lloyds

503. PAPAGO TERRITORY
GNG, No. 15; Beaux Arts Gallerie, San Francisco, 1928; HDMG, 1933; P2L; illus. *San Francisco News*, early May 1928; possibly CPLH, No. 61, CACTUS GARDEN

504. PASQUAL(E)
Watercolor
HDMG, 1940, No. 12

505. PATAGONIA
Painting
GNG, No. 5; Tucson, Arizona, newspaper, exact title unknown, March 25, 1928 (review)

506. PEAR BLOSSOMS
HDMG, 1933

507. PEAR TREES
SAG

508. PENITENTE MARADA [sic]
Maybe same as MARADA, see No. 467 here
Probably an oil painting
1931E; CAA (year ?)

509. POOL
Painting
KG, No. 2; GNG, No. 21; D-WG, 1931; *Carmelite*, Mar. 26, 1931; 1931E

510. PORTRAIT: MARTIN FLAVIN
Known to have been painted, information courtesy Russell Williams

511. PORTRAIT: MEXICAN
Oil painting
Albert M. Bender Collection (from F. Perret files. See n. 273)

512. PORTRAIT: ELLA YOUNG
Watercolor
CAA, 1945. See discussion of this work in text p. 124

513. PORTRAIT STUDY
Charcoal
CPLH, No. 45

514. PROSPECTOR'S PARADISE
GNG, No. 17; HDMG, 1933

515. PUBLIC LAUNDRY
Painting
HDMG, 1936, No. 14

516. RED GIANTS
Painting
KG, No. 17

517. RESPECTABILITY
Charcoal
D-WG, 1933; CPLH, No. 43

518. ROCK
Charcoal
D-WG, 1933

519. ROCKS AND FOG
Oil painting
34 × 40
MEC, No. 2

520. ROYAL GORGE
Painting
HGSF, No. 5

521. ROYAL PALMS
SAG; HDMG, 1933; MPH, Sept. 14, 1933

522. RUSTY CYPRESS
Probably an oil painting
First Prize 87th Annual State Fair, Sacramento, 1941, Catalogue No. 41

523. SALT MARSHES
Painting
GNG, No. 26; critique, Tucson, Arizona, newspaper, exact title unknown, Mar. 25, 1928; CPLH, No. 19

524. SAND ARABESQUE
Charcoal
CPLH, No. 36

525. SAN GABRIEL'S PASS
Painting
HGSF, No. 19

526. SCULPTURED COAST
Painting
GNG, No. 22

527. SCULPTURE
(Study for carving ?)
Charcoal
D-WG, 1933; CPLH, No. 58

528. SEA AND SKY
Oil painting (?)
LGC, *The Gallery*, March 1965, No. 23

529. SEA FANTASY
Charcoal
D-WG, 1933; CPLH, No. 41; CAA, 1934; CPC, Oct. 19, 1934

530. SEA LACE
Watercolor
HDMG, 1940, No. 8

531. SEAL COVE
Painting
GNG, No. 25

532. SEARED HILLS IN SUNLIGHT
Probably an oil painting
HGP

533. SEVENTEEN MILE DRIVE
1931E

534. SHELTERED COVE
Oil painting
20 × 24
MEC, No. 12

535. SIESTA
Oil painting
FMC; LAT, May 9, 1915; HDMG, 1936, No. 10; CAA (year ?)

536. SILVER SCREEN (BIRCHES ?)
Oil painting
FMC; LAT, May 9, 1915

537. SMUGGLER'S COVE
Painting
HGSF, No. 14; HDMG, 1940

538. SONOMA WINERY BARNS
Probably a watercolor or drawing
25 × 33
Initialed J.O'S. Label extant

539. SOUL OF LINCOLN STEFFENS
("Imaginative painting in color")
D-WG, 1933; illus. in n. 235
Black/white print extant

540. SOUTH OF SUR
D-WG, 1931; CPC, Oct. 12, 1934

541. SPECULATIONS
Charcoal
D-WG, 1933

542. SPRING
FMC; LAT, May 9, 1915

543. SPRING
Painting
HGSF, No. 18

544. SPRING
Colored wood block (?)
CAA, 1945. See n. 291

545. SPRING FANTASY
Painting
GNG, No. 18

546. SPRING IN THE SALINAS VALLEY
Probably an oil painting
CAA, 1937; CPC, Sept. 10, 1937

547. SPRING MOONLIGHT
Painting
HGSF, No. 1. See No. 481 here

548. STILL LIFE
Probably an oil painting
CAA (year ?)

549. STREAM
Oil painting
Society for Sanity in Art at the CPLH, Nov. 1, 1941– Jan. 4, 1942

550. STREET SWEEPER
Painting
HDMG, 1936, No. 9

551. STUDY FOR CARVING
D-WG, 1933

552. SUBMARINE
Painting
HDMG, 1933

553. SUBMARINE GARDEN
Charcoal
1931E; D-WG, 1933

554. SUBMARINE GARDEN
Painting
CPLH, No. 31

555. SUN DIAL
Oil painting
FMC; LAT, May 9, 1915

556. SUNSET ON OLD BALDY
Oil painting
FMC. Could be either Maine or California.

557. SUPERSTITION MOUNTAINS
(later MAGIC MOUNTAINS)
Painting
GNG, No. 1. See Nos. 25, 67 here

558. SURPRISED
Oil painting
FMC

559. SUSPIRING SEA (SUSPIRING SURGE)
Watercolor
HDMG, 1940, No. 11; MPH, Sept. 24, 1940; Statewide Exh., Santa Cruz, 1943, No. 73

560. TABBIE (TAFFIE ?)
Charcoal
D-WG, 1933

561. TAHITIAN BOY (TAHITIAN YOUTH)
Charcoal
D-WG, 1933; MPH, Mar. 9, 1933; CPLH, No. 35

562. TAHITIAN DANCE
Charcoal
D-WG, 1933; MPH, Mar. 9, 1933; CPLH, No. 56, lent by Mrs. Abraham Rosenberg

563. TAHITIAN VILLAGE
Smaller canvas
CAA; CPC, Nov. 23, 1934

564. TAOS GIRL (INDIAN GIRL ?)
22L

565. TAOS INDIAN ("Green Coat")
Oil painting
HDMG, 1933; Nelson Gallery, Kansas City, 1937

566. THREE FIGURES ON A QUAY
Probably an oil painting
HGP

567. THREE TREES
LAMA, 1919, No. 30
Lent by Miss Augusta Senter

568. TIERRA DEL FUEGO
GNG, No. 4; LAT, Feb. 5, 1928

569. TORRE DE VIENTO
Painting
GNG, No. 8

570. TRANQUILIDAD (SQUATTING MAN)
Painting
HDMG, 1936, No. 6

571. TREASURE ISLAND
Painting
KG, No. 16

572. TREE FORMS
Watercolor (gouache)
22½ × 30½
MEC, No. 22

573. TREES
LAMA, 1921, No. 41
Lent by Miss Augusta Senter

574. TREE STRAINING OUT OF THE ROCK
Charcoal
CAA, 1945

575. TREES IN SPRING
Oil painting
FMC

576. TREE TRUNK
Oil painting (?)
LGC, *The Gallery*, March 1965, No. 22

577. TROPIC LANDSCAPE
Oil on canvas
Nelson Gallery, Kansas City, 1937

578. TROPICAL LANDSCAPE
(Description: "A lush tropical landscape")
CAA; CPC, Mar. 8, 1935

579. TRUNK OF OLD CYPRESS (CYPRESS)
D-WG, 1933

580. "TWO STRIKING PAINTINGS IN GESSO"
CAA; CPC, May 20, 1938. See p. 113

581. URINATION OF CARE, ca. 1941
Mixed media (?)
5 ft. × 4 ft. (?)
Signed LL
Cartoon for Bohemian Club Grove

582. VAQUERO
Painting
HDMG, 1936, No. 4

583. VIEW
(Description: "View from his window—Tahiti")
Ella Winter in *Carmelite*. See n. 196

584. WAN WOMAN
D-WG, 1933; CPLH, No. 50

585. WET DAY HONOLULU
Oil on canvas
Nelson Gallery, Kansas City, 1937

586. WILD HORSE
Charcoal
D-WG, 1933; CPLH, No. 54, lent by Edward Weston

587. WIND LYRE
Watercolor
HDMG, 1940

588. WINEBIBBER
Watercolor
CPLH, No. 62

589. WINTER
Oil painting
FMC

590. WOMAN OF TAXCO
Painting
HDMC, 1936, No. 7

591. WORLD IN THE MAKING
Tucson, Arizona newspaper, exact title unknown, Mar. 25, 1928

592. YELLOW CALLAS (CALLA LILIES)
SAG; HDMG, 1933; CPLH, No. 1; CPC, Mar. 8, 1935; CAA (year ?)
Early photograph by Lewis Josselyn, Carmel extant.

MEMBERSHIP

In chronological order; year(s) when first mentioned or known:

California Art Club, Los Angeles, California, 1914
Carmel Club of Arts and Crafts, 1917
San Francisco Art Association, 1918
Society of Independent Artists, New York, New York, 1922
American Watercolor Society, 1922–1941
Carmel Art Association, 1927
    A branch of American Artists Professional League after 1941
San Francisco Bay Region Art Association, 1939
Society for Sanity in Art, 1941
    Later Society of Western Artists
Bohemian Club, San Francisco, California, 1941
The New Group, Monterey Peninsula, California, 1951

INSTITUTIONAL COLLECTIONS

Bohemian Club, San Francisco, California
City Hall, Carmel-by-the-Sea, California
Harrison Memorial Library, Carmel, California
Mills College Art Gallery, Oakland, California
Monterey Peninsula Museum of Art, Monterey, California
Museum of Modern Art, Dublin, Ireland
Sheldon Swope Art Gallery, Terre Haute, Indiana

Chronology of John O'Shea's Life

1876 — O'Shea is born in Ballintaylor, Dungarvan, County Waterford, Ireland, of Patrick Shea and Catherine Egan. He is baptized October 15 as John Shea.

ca. 1882– ca. 1890 — O'Shea attends school in Ballintaylor; perhaps also in Cork and Dublin.

ca. 1890 — Goes to New York City.

ca. 1890–1913 — Studies possibly with Charles Harry Eaton in Leonia, New Jersey, and sometime during this period at Art Students League, for one year with George B. Bridgman; at Adelphi Academy with John Barnard Whittaker for two years. Paints in Maine.

1907–1913 — Lives in Brooklyn. Listed as artist at 32 Union Square East and at 132 East Twenty-third near Lexington Avenue in Manhattan.

1911–1912 — Works at Tiffany and Company, New York.

1912 — Probably meets future wife Molly Donally Crawford Shaughnessy in New York.

1913 — Goes to Pasadena, opens studio. Exhibits large number of paintings at studio of Kenneth Avery in Pasadena and at Friday Morning Club, Los Angeles. Lauded by critic Antony Anderson.

1914 — Exhibits at Hotel Green, Pasadena. Contributes to relief fund for European artists with California Art Club at Blanchard Gallery, Los Angeles.

1915 — Exhibits again at Friday Morning Club, Los Angeles. Lauded by critic Beatric de Lack Krombach. O'Shea's studio is at 657 Oakland Avenue, Pasadena.

1916 — Shares studio/home at Laguna Beach, California, with future wife Molly. First mention of being in Carmel, California, October 27, arriving "from Los Angeles."

1917 — Goes to Carmel but apparently retains studio in Pasadena, arriving, however, "from New York" in November.

1918 — In January first exhibition in Carmel; in March exhibits at the Forty-third Annual of the San Francisco Art Association (SFAA).

1919 — One-man show at Helgesen Gallery, San Francisco.

1919–1921 — Shows at Summer Exhibitions, Los Angeles County Museum.

1920 — Exhibits at Forty-fourth Annual of the SFAA.

1921 — Large one-man show at Kingore Galleries, New York. O'Shea lives at Sherwood Studios, New York.

1922 — Shows at Sixth Annual Exhibition of The Society of Independent Artists, New York; work lauded by critic Royal Cortissoz. Marries Molly Shaughnessy in New York. European honeymoon.

1923 — O'Sheas settle in Carmel Highlands and begin building their house "Tynalacan." He retains quarters at Sherwood Studios, New York. Painting again, getting ready for winter exhibitions. Winter in Pasadena after sojourning in Pebble Beach, California.

1924 — Shows at Annual Exhibition by Artists of Carmel. Winter in Pasadena.

1925 — Molly O'Shea spends three months in New York City.

1925–1927 — O'Shea takes painting trips to Arizona, sometimes with friend and painter Theodore Criley.

1926 — Shows at art gallery of newly opened Hotel San Carlos, Monterey, California.

1927 — Initial meeting of Carmel Art Association (CAA) and formal opening of new art gallery where O'Shea shows. Joins artists in sale of paintings on "time plan" at East West Gallery, San Francisco.

1928 — Shows at Hotel Del Monte Art Gallery, Monterey (HDMG) and Pasadena Art Institute. Large one-man show at Grace Nicholson Galleries, Pasadena; Temple Art Gallery, Tucson, Arizona; and Beaux Arts Galerie, San Francisco. Lauded by Arthur Millier. Is juror of traveling exhibition of CAA. O'Sheas journey to South Pacific.

1929 — Juror, CAA exhibit.

1930 — O'Shea, a British subject by birth, becomes U.S. citizen in San Francisco. Fellow artist and best friend Theodore Criley dies suddenly. Probably painting in Arizona and New Mexico during winter.

1931 — Shows at CAA. Exhibits painting and sculpture at Monterey County Fair. Large one-man show at Denny-Watrous Gallery (D-WG), Carmel. Lauded by Edward Weston. Exhibits at Fifty-third Annual SFAA. Spends winter in New York and Chicago.

1932 Shows "huge and sombre portrait" at the CAA annual. Selected as "active fireman" in Carmel Highlands district. Is part of Carmel's own "Hall of Fame" as artist. Shows two "grotesque masses of ink" at CAA exhibit at D-WG.

1933 Large one-man exhibition of charcoal drawings at D-WG. Shows at Annual Exhibition of Works of Western Artists, Oakland Art Gallery. Large one-man exhibition at HDMG and Thomas Welton Stanford Gallery at Stanford University, Palo Alto, California. Lauded by Josephine Mildred Blanch.

1934 Signs as Director of CAA when it incorporates. Large one-man exhibition at California Palace of the Legion of Honor, San Francisco. Lauded by Junius Cravens. Opening exhibition of new D-WG; large one-man show. Exhibition of small paintings at CAA.

1935 Several shows at CAA, now on nearly a monthly schedule. Watercolor exhibition in January is particularly noteworthy. Large one-man exhibition by invitation of Kingsley Art Club at E. B. Crocker Art Gallery, Sacramento, California. O'Sheas spend six months in Mexico.

1936 Large one-man exhibition at HDMG featuring Mexican subjects. Lauded by Blanch Mathias. Shows at spring and fall exhibitions at the San Francisco Museum of Art. The O'Sheas winter in Indiana, Florida, and New York.

1937 Elected President of CAA. Loan Exhibition, William Rockhill Nelson Gallery of Art, Kansas City, Missouri. O'Shea's large painting, *Comida, Market Day*, installed at Harrison Memorial Library, Carmel. Shows at CAA in several monthly shows and with the CAA at Stanford University for one exhibition. Prize paintings offered by O'Shea, Paul Dougherty, William Ritschel, Armin Hansen in drawing at CAA for building fund.

1938 Shows at several of the monthly exhibits of the CAA and at the first exhibition by the CAA at Salinas, California. O'Shea's watercolors at the May exhibition of the CAA are striking. O'Shea is re-elected president of the CAA; his work "dominates the August exhibitions." "The Hansen, The Ritschel and The Great O'Shea" poem is published. The O'Sheas move to Pebble Beach.

1939 Shows at Golden Gate International Exposition, California Building, Treasure Island in San Francisco Bay; at California State Fair in Sacramento and in the Fifth Annual Exhibition of Artist Members of Bay Region Art Association at Oakland Art Gallery.

1940 Shows another painting at extended Golden Gate International Exhibition on Treasure Island in *Committees and Juries* exhibition. Watercolors by O'Shea and oils by Burton S. Boundey shown at closing of HDMG. Shows again at Oakland Art Gallery for Bay Region Art Association.

1941 Molly O'Shea dies of cancer at St. Luke's Hospital in San Francisco. O'Shea becomes artist-member in Bohemian Club, San Francisco; goes to Club's Grove encampment. Shows at California Palace of the Legion of Honor in Exhibition by San Francisco Branch of Society for Sanity in Art. Shows at California State Fair, Sacramento; wins first prize, second prize goes to Paul Dougherty, third to Nick Brigante. CAA joins American Artists Professional League.

1942 Shows at Bohemian Club, San Francisco. Works are lauded by Alfred Frankenstein. Continues active in CAA. O'Shea moves to "Masten house" in Carmel Highlands.

1943 Shows at State-wide Art Exhibition, Santa Cruz, California.

183. STROLLER, cat. no. 238.

1944 O'Shea moves for the last time—to Carmel Woods.

1946 Portrait of Ella Young exhibited at Grand Central Galleries, New York (?).

1946–1950 Exhibits collections of paintings, annually except 1949, at local establishments in celebration of "Art Week."

1951 Joins and exhibits with "New Group" in Monterey.

1952–1955 Shows sporadically works at CAA. Last review known is by Irene Alexander, lauding "high standards," March 1955.

1956 Dies in Carmel Woods home on April 29. Memorial exhibition in October at CAA arranged by Richard M. Lofton.

1963–1967 Exhibitions and sales at The Laky Galleries, Carmel, which represent the estate.

1983 WIM Fine Arts, Oakland, California, acquires O'Shea estate from family.

1986 Retrospective exhibitions planned to open at Monterey Peninsula Museum of Art, January 17, and the Civic Arts Gallery, Walnut Creek, California, November 5.

Certificate of Authenticity

STATE OF CALIFORNIA) ss.
COUNTY OF MONTEREY)

    EMMA L. PINE, being duly sworn, says:

    That she was the sister-in-law of John O'Shea, now deceased; that she is the distributee under the last will of John O'Shea, deceased of all paintings, sketches and works of art created by John O'Shea, deceased, and has had, and now has the actual possession of such paintings, sketches and works of art; that she was acquainted with the works of John O'Shea for a period of more than 40 years prior to his death;

    That among the paintings, sketches and works of John O'Shea, deceased are many unsigned paintings, sketches and works of art; that she has examined the work of art to which this affidavit is attached and which is not signed by John O'Shea, deceased, and that she knows of her own knowledge that said work is the work of John O'Shea, now deceased, and that the same has been in her possession or control since the death of John O'Shea.

Emma L. Pine

Subscribed and sworn to before me
this 28th day of September, 1960

Carmel C. Martin, Jr.
Carmel C. Martin, Jr.
Notary Public in and for the County
of Monterey, State of California

Estate Stamps

As indicated in the text, John O'Shea did not sign many of his works. In a variety of media, whether on stretched canvas or on other support such as cardboard or paper, all of the unsigned works which were obtained from the estate of the artist by WIM Fine Arts, Oakland, in 1983, have been marked with an estate stamp, suitable to the work.

    The following are facsimiles of those estate stamps:

On oil paintings primarily, front

JOHN O'SHEA

On drawings, watercolors, and sketches, front

John O'Shea   *John O'Shea*

On the reverse of all the estate stamped works appears the stamp

Afterword and Acknowledgments

When this book was originally contemplated we planned to present only a picture book with commentary by art critics who were contemporaries of John O'Shea. Not an original idea, to be sure, but one that appealed to us from the standpoint of overall conciseness and precise knowledge expressed by art experts. However, it was soon discovered that most of what had been said and written about John O'Shea the person was fraught with faults and fantasies perpetuated in most instances by copying or verbally repeating wrong dates and events pertinent to the life and works of the artist.

It seemed appropriate, therefore, to start at the beginning and present as complete a biographical chronology as possible, using information drawn from extant original documents or letters and interspersing commentaries and anecdotes by persons who knew the artist personally. An attempt was made to weed out mistakes by locating primary sources of information recorded as close chronologically as possible to particular dates and events of interest.

Newspaper accounts, catalogues, checklists, price lists, critics' comments, etc., were compared with each other and served to establish specific dates of exhibitions and the original name of many of the paintings. However, as with many written documents, and especially with the spoken word, errors do occur. The same was noted in direct interviews with persons who knew John O'Shea, albeit thirty years or more ago—memory having failed or been embellished in retrospect.

It is obvious from the preceding that many persons, some representing public or private institutions, had to be consulted and their help, understanding, and support is gratefully acknowledged with the finished work.

In hope that there are no omissions and to indicate the extent to which involvement with such a work can lead, we attempt to list all of the participants in this endeavor—noting in particular the efforts of Joseph Armstrong Baird, Jr., and Suzanne Chun, who helped to edit the final manuscript.

Rachel M. Allen, Assistant Chief, Office of Research Support, Smithsonian Institution, Washington, D.C.; Martha Shipman Andrews, Coordinator, Inventory of American Paintings, Smithsonian Institution, Washington, D.C.; Archives of California Art, The Oakland Museum, California; The Art Institute of Chicago; Mr. and Mrs. John Barry, Ballintaylor, Dungarvan, Ireland; Diane Bayless, Assistant Registrar, The Sheldon Swope Art Gallery, Terre Haute, Indiana; Shelley M. Bennett, Associate Curator, The Huntington Library, San Marino, California; William Henry Black, Sonoma, California; Richard M. Blaney, Carmel, California; Mr. Keith Brehmer, Reference Librarian, The Harrison Memorial Library, Carmel, California; Jennifer Bright, Photo Librarian, Museum of the City of New York; Gary Breitweiser, Studio 2, Santa Barbara, California; Peter W. Brown, Assistant Curator, Civic Arts Gallery, Walnut Creek, California; Helen Bruton, Monterey, California; Adeline Bua, Development Office, Adelphi Academy, Brooklyn, New York; Charles F. Bulotti,

Jr., Past President, Bohemian Club of San Francisco, San Mateo, California; William Callanan, Parish Priest, Aglish, County Waterford, Ireland; Paul T. Carey, Piedmont, California; Helen B. Christensen, Pebble Beach, California; Renato Contini, First Vice President, California Art Club, Los Angeles; Charles Coon, Gloucester, Massachusetts; Lisa Dougherty Coon, Gloucester, Massachusetts; Nancy Couto, Manager, Subsidiary Rights, Cornell University Press, Ithaca, New York; Richard Criley, Carmel, California; Roy Dahlstrom, Engineering Office, Fort Ord, California; Jeramyn Davern, Grand Central Galleries, New York; William and Grace Davis, Palo Alto, California; Doris Ostrander Dawdy, San Francisco; Barbara Dawson, Rights and Reproductions, National Gallery of Ireland, Dublin; Rick Deragon, Assistant Curator/Registrar, Monterey Peninsula Museum of Art, Monterey, California; John J. Devine, London, England; Ann Dickman-Grant, Federal Way, Washington; Gael Donovan, Carmel Art Association, Carmel, California; Marty Drickey, Museum Administrator, Stanford University Museum of Art, Palo Alto, California; Micaela Martinez DuCasse, Piedmont, California; Allison M. Eckardt, Associate Editor, *The Magazine Antiques*, New York; Marianna Eisner, Museum Registrar, Laguna Beach Museum of Art, California; Mrs. Electa H. Elphand, Mill Valley, California; Rowland Elzea, Associate Director, Delaware Art Museum, Wilmington; Marion D. Engstrom, Assistant Director, Sunset Center, Carmel, California; D. Kirke Erskine, Carmel, California; Jeannette Parkes Ewing, Carmel, California; Sandi Farrel, City Hall, Carmel-by-the-Sea, California; Sheila Fielding, Registrar, South Eastern Health Board, St. Patrick's Hospital, Waterford, Ireland; The Fieldstone Company, Newport Beach, California; Mr. and Mrs. Sean Flavin, Monterey, California; Rosina A. Florio, Executive Director, The Art Students League of New York; Norman Mcd. Foster, Carmel, California; Miss Duane Garrison, Divisional Vice President, Cultural Affairs, Tiffany and Company, New York; Robert Godfrey, American Visuals, Inc., Terre Haute, Indiana; Reeve Gould, Berkeley, California; Heather Hendrickson, Registrar/Curatorial Assistant, Laguna Beach Museum of Art, California; Cdr. and Mrs. W. D. Hoot, Carmel, California; Brian Hourican, Something Special, Oakland, California; John Langley Howard, San Francisco; Annette Hughes, Volunteer, Photo Services, The Fine Arts Museums of San Francisco; Edan Hughes, San Francisco; Mr. and Mrs. William G. Hughes, Palos Verdes Estates, California; Mrs. Warren M. Hussey, Terre Haute, Indiana; Mr. and Mrs. William G. Hyland, Monterey, California; Consulate General of Ireland, San Francisco; Loren G. Janzen, Carmel Art Association, Carmel, California; Dan and Lilith James, Carmel, California; Dr. Andrew G. Jameson, Archivist, Bohemian Club, San Francisco; Richard, Molly, and Sally Jeppson, Carmel, California; Jane Johnson, Raleigh, North Carolina; Samantha Johnston, Museum Technician, Registrar's Office, National Gallery of Art, Washington, D.C.; Nan and Roy Farrington Jones, Early California and Western Art Research, Ross, California; Robert D. Kinsman, Director, The Sheldon Swope Art Gallery, Terre Haute, Indiana; Mrs. Lawrence W. Kirkhart, Membership Secretary, Friday Morning Club of Los Angeles, Santa Monica, California; Molly Knox, Terre Haute, Indiana; Gabriela Knubis, Director, Public Relations, Monterey Sheraton, Monterey, California; Dr. and Mrs. Edward Krug, Oakland, California; Gyöngy Laky, San Francisco; Les Laky, Carmel, California; Thomas V. Lange, Assistant Curator of Rare Books, The Huntington Library, San Marino, California; Thomas Layton, San Francisco; Emma-Rose Layton, Carmel, California; Janet J. LeClair, New York; Lee LeMaster, Director, Officers' Club, Fort Ord, California; Irene Chapellier Little, Director, Chapellier Galleries, Inc., New York; Thomas J. Logan, Director, Monterey Peninsula Museum of Art, Monterey, California; Mrs. George H. Macy, Carmel, California; Evelyn R. Manning, Chief, Records Management and Research Division, Office of Management, Bureau of Personnel, United States Department of State, Washington, D.C.;

Lajos Markos, Houston, Texas; Erik Martin, Something Special, Oakland, California; Tim and Lynn Mason, Carmel, California; Betty Hoag McGlynn, Art Historian, Archivist and former Research Director, Carmel Museum of Art, Carmel, California; William McNaught, Director, New York Area, Smithsonian Institution, Archives of American Art, New York; Paul Messer Antiques, Moss Landing, California; Lorna and John Meyer, Piedmont, California; Diane Migliori, Program Director, Stilwell Recreation Center, Fort Ord, California; Sally Mills, Curator, Vassar College Art Gallery, Poughkeepsie, New York; Mills College Art Gallery, Oakland, California; James F. Morris, Tacoma, Washington; Joe Moure, Pasadena, California; National Academy of Design, New York; Margye Neswitz, Pebble Beach, California, former Editor, *Members Memo*, Monterey Peninsula Museum of Art; Reference Librarian and General Research Division, The New York Public Library, Fifth Avenue at 42nd Street, New York; Newspaper Room, Main Library, University of California, Berkeley; Newspaper Room, Public Library, Oakland, California; C. P. Noblet, Internist, Reference Department, State Public Library, Sacramento, California; Timothy Nolan, Assistant, Library Archivist, Whitney Museum of American Art, New York; Mrs. John O'Meara, Carmel, California; Barbara Orbach, Library Intern, Art Research Library, Los Angeles County Museum of Art; Margaret Pelikan, Director, The Harrison Memorial Library, Carmel, California; Bennard B. Perlman, Baltimore, Maryland; Helen L. Pinkney, Librarian, The Dayton Art Institute, Ohio; Mr. and Mrs. James Pruitt, Carmel, California; Debra L. Pughe, Exhibition Manager, The Fine Arts Museums of San Francisco; M. H. deYoung Memorial Museum, San Francisco; Jerry Pullen, City Hall, Carmel-by-the-Sea, California; Mrs. Alan Purchase, Los Altos, California; Bruce A. Reeves, Assessor, Monterey County, Salinas, California; Jane H. Renner, Terre Haute, Indiana; Sheldon Rothblatt, Professor of History, University of California, Berkeley; Dr. Charles Adams Rowe, Piedmont, California; Spokesperson for Samoans for Samoans of California, Inc., San Francisco; Jacqueline Samols, Photographic Archives, Sotheby's, New York; Miss Helen Sanger, Frick Art Reference Library, New York; Edward C. Saunders, Atlanta, Georgia; Kent Seavey, Pacific Grove, California; Don Shorts, Ventura, California; Cynthia Cobb Snyder, Reference Services, Pasadena Public Library, California; Gordon and Joan Spencer, Soquel, California; Mr. Jean Stern, Director, Petersen Galleries, Beverly Hills, California; John Sullivan, Lakeport, California; Michael Sullivan, Santa Ana, California; Robert J. Tipler, M.D., Centralia, Washington; Ms. Mariann Touba, Librarian, The New York Historical Society; Rose Ulman, Carmel, California; Ethna Waldron, Curator, The Hugh Lane Municipal Gallery of Modern Art, Dublin, Ireland; William B. Walker, Chief Librarian, Thomas J. Watson Library, The Metropolitan Museum of Art, New York; Sally Waterman, European Paintings, The Metropolitan Museum of Art, New York; Ruth Westphal, President, Westphal Publishing, Newport Beach, California; Cynthia Criley Williams, Carmel, California; John Garrett Williams, Carmel, California; Russell D. Williams, M.D., Monterey, California; Estate of Donald Winston (James T. Wyman, Executor), Minneapolis, Minnesota; Mr. and Mrs. Anthony R. White, Hillsborough, California; Carl Worth, Director/Curator, Civic Arts Gallery, Walnut Creek, California; Dr. and Mrs. Sydney T. Wright, Selma, California.